Ferruccio Canali

PADUA

History and Masterpieces

244 Colour illustrations
Map of the city
5 Itineraries

BONECHI EDIZIONI "IL TURISMO" FIRENZE

© Copyright 1996 by Bonechi Edizioni "Il Turismo" S.r.l.
Via dei Rustici, 5 - 50122 Florence
Phone: (055) 239 82 24/25 - Fax: (055) 21 63 66

Photographs: from the Bonechi Edizioni "Il Turismo" archives (page 3)
           Paolo Bacherini
           K&B News: pp. 5 - 10 - 11 - 13 - 71 - 72 - 73
           Giorgio Deganello: pp. 6 - 12 (bottom) - 14 - 15 - 16 - 17
           - 18 - 19 - 20 - 21
           I-Buga Sas. Milano: pp. 35 (top) - 56 (bottom) - 85
Layout by: Barbara Bonechi
Cover Design by: Claudia Baggiani
Translation: Julia Weiss
Photolithography by: La Fotolitografia, Florence
Printed by: Lito Terrazzi, Florence
ISBN 88-7204-236-4

A view of the city.

HISTORICAL NOTES

Padua, inhabited since the end of the X century B.C., became an important center of Venetic civilization sometime around the VI century B.C. as borne out by the evidence uncovered in the fine nearby necropoles. The pieces found there are now in the Museo Civico degli Eremitani

In the I century B.C. it became a Roman city and was rebuilt with a network of parallel and perpendicular streets (the cardo-decumanus structure). It was a very important civitas not only in the Padania region, but also within the context of the links between Rome and the Eastern provinces of the Empire. The ruins of the **Arena** *date from when the city was Romanized like the* **Teatro Zairo**, *its counterpart on the other side of the city where the Prato della Valle is today. Naturally, there are other fine mosaics and sculptures from that period as well, and these are in the Museo Civico degli Eremitani. Padua, therefore, was culturally important in addition to playing a key political-economic role: the great Roman historian Livy was born there (59 B.C.).*

From the early Christian period there is the chapel or **sacellum of Saint Prosdocimo** *in the church of Santa Giustina near the Prato della Valle. In 601 the city was razed to the ground by the Longobards; the devastation was so complete that the outskirts of the city reverted to swampland and the inhabitants moved away from the town center in search of safer areas.*

The city began to prosper in the XI century. Its wealth was evident in 1232 when the **Basilica of Saint Anthony** *was founded, and by the fact that there were 130 towers. In 1237 Padua was controlled by Ezzelino da Romano, who allied himself with Frederick II and welcomed him to the city two years later. He remained in power until the League, led by Pope Alexander IV drove Ezzelino from Padua and reestablished communal freedoms. Shortly before this event, in 1222 a group of students and professors who had left the University of Bologna came to Padua and established what along with the University of Bologna is one of the world's oldest institutions of higher learning.*

The city flourished during the XIV century and expanded to control nearby towns as well. Then, in 1318 Jacopo da Carrara became the Capitano Generale.

This meant the end of the communal regime and the start of battles and power struggles against Venice, Verona and Milan. In the meantime, at the beginning of the XIV century, Giotto frescoed the **Cappella degli Scrovegni** *(known as the Arena Chapel) (1305) as well as some important walls in the "Santo" and in the Palazzo della Ragione. He was followed by Giusto de' Menabuoi (who worked mainly in the baptistry) and Altichiero Veronese, thereby launching that important period in Paduan painting that was also one of the highlights of Medieval Art.*

In 1371 the city's cultural panorama was enhanced by the presence of Francesco Petrarca (Petrarch) who was a guest of the Carrara family.

In 1405 Padua was occupied by the Venetians and was to remain part of the "Serenissima" until the treaty of Campoformio was signed in 1797.

Donatello's works date from the XV century, starting with the altar in the Basilica of Sant'Antonio. The one we see today, however, is a partial reconstruction of the original.

Donatello was followed by Francesco Squarcione and his school, Andrea Mantegna and the Lombardo brothers who created masterpieces of humanistic art.

In the sixteenth century, when the Paduan nobles were starting to obtain important positions in the government of the Venetian Republic, and mainly when the Venetian aristocracy began investing resources in the mainland, Padua became a crucial nerve center in the Serenissma.

The greatest artists in the Republic created masterpieces in the city, from Falconetto and his school, from Sansovino to Sanmicheli to Titian; from Campagnola to the Florentine Bartolommeo Ammannati who had close relationships with the Mantova-Benavides family, from Palladio a native son, although there are no works in the city that can be definitely attributed to him, to Andrea Maroni.

This great artistic commitment was to last through the coming centuries with the works of Padovanino and then Vincenzo Scamozzi, the Bonazza family of great sculptors and Canova who worked on the Prato della Valle.

After the French occupation during Napoleon's Italian Campaign, Padua as a city in the Lombard-Veneto province was ceded to Austria.

In 1848 the Paduans joined in the uprisings until 1866 when the city officially became part of the Kingdom of Italy.

The ruins of the Arena and the façade of the Chapel of the Scrovegni; below: *the Sacello of San Prosdocimo, Basilica of Santa Giustina.*

In the nineteenth century an important school of architects flourished in the city. They were an eclectic group with an historicist imprint that reproposed styles from the past with a new look. Giuseppe Jappelli, for example intelligently and skillfully reproposed all historical styles after much careful study of the originals, from the Neodoric to the Neoetruscan, from the Neoegyptian to the Neogothic. Then there was Camillo Boito, one of the most important founders of modern sensibility connected to the problems of restorations and philological restoration of the original elements of the historic buildings.

*From the early twentieth century there are the works of Giò Ponti, Massimo Campigli and Gino Severini who did the fine paintings in the new **Palazzo dell'Università**, and those by Torres which are among the earliest examples of Rationalist art in Italy. Unfortunately, during World War II Padua, an important strategic center, suffered massive bombing raids and lost fine monuments such as the apse of the **Church of the Eremitani** which was philologically reconstructed on the basis of the sensiibility propounded decades earlier by Camillo Boito.*

*Although Padua, with its old porticoed streets, projects an image of an old city, it is not lacking some fine modern buildings such as the **Pediatric Hospital of the University** designed by Daniele Calabi (1951-52) on the basis of research on European functionalism started in the 'thirties, the **Fair Building** by Giuseppe Davanzo (1965-68) which alludes to an enormous tent linking open and closed spaces; the new headquarters of the **Banca d'Italia** in Via Roma-Riviera Tito Livio by the Samonà brothers (1968-1974) with its indoor gallery and great emphasis on the relationship between the old city and modern architecture; and finally the **Museo Civico** and the **Pinacoteca degli Eremitani** (1969-1985) by Albini, Helg and Piva distinguished by the staircase made of octagonal elements and the interior decor in spite of the fact that it stands alongside of the church of the Eremitani. The building is still a skeleton structure and may shortly be torn down because it clashes strongly with the old urban landscape. It has led to bitter debate that has in turn put Padua back into the cultural limelight due to the issue of the relationship between ancient and modern within the historic city.*

Francesco Squarcione, the De Lazara Polyptych, Museo Civico degli Eremitani.

Next page: ***Chapel of the Scrovegni, or the Arena Chapel, general view of the altar.***

Railroad Station and **Corso del Popolo**
Roman Arena (*Corso Garibaldi / piazza degli Eremitani*)
Museo Civico degli Eremitani (*piazza degli Eremitani*)
Chapel of the Annunciation or **degli Scrovegni,**
or **Arena Chapel** (*piazza degli Eremitani*)
Church of the Eremitani (*piazza degli Eremitani*)
Palazzo Mantova-Benavides (*piazza degli Eremitani*)
Public Slaughterhouse (*via Loredan*)
Church of San Gaetano (*via Altinate*)
Church of Santa Sofia
Mocenigo-Querini Palace (*via Sant'Eufemia*)
Lando-Correr Court (*via Gabelli*)
Church of San Francesco (*via San Francesco*)
Porta Pontecorvo or **Liviana** (*piazzale Pontecorvo*)
Cornaro Loggia and **Odeum** (*via Cesarotti*)

Railroad Station

①

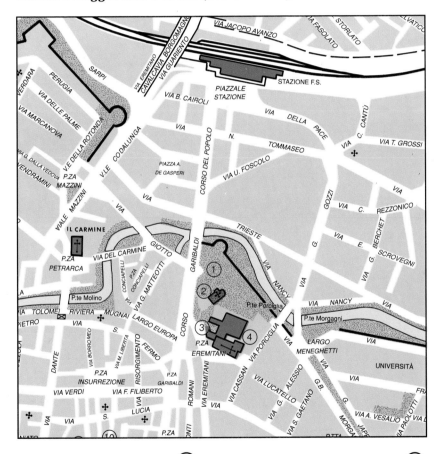

②

③

④

RAILROAD STATION AND CORSO DEL POPOLO

Corso del Popolo.

The beautiful railroad station that was rebuilt in the nineteen thirties consists of a large central body, with big vertical openings and a protruding platform that create a sheltered waiting area for the passengers. On either side of this core, there are two symmetrical wings with a series of 11 slim columns that extend to both stories of the building (something of a giant, modern order). They recall a simplified Doric style without a proper base and are topped by very essential beams.

The **Corso del Popolo** is a broad avenue; the part closest to the station is pure twentieth century with its impressive buidings. At the corner of Piazza Stazione is the *Grande Albergo Italia*, an Art Déco structure with iron floral motifs on the railings and planters. After a series of eclectic late XIX century buildings, facing Piazza De Gasperi, we come to the Foro (market) with a low façade of rough stone and huge reliefs protruding from below the round openings (under restoration since 1994).

Railroad Station.

The ruins of the Roman Arena.

Two views of the Arena Gardens and *the bust of Ruzante (1496-1542), playwright and actor;* (below) *the Arena Chapel.*

THE ROMAN ARENA

The eliptical **Arena**,a typical amphitheater with a base of eighty arches, is the single greatest vestige of the Roman presence in Padua during the Flavian era (60-70 A.D.). As in other cities, this enormous structure dedicated to the "mass entertainment" of the day, was built at the edge of the city, neatly counterbalancing the city's theater (Zairo) that stood on the site of what is now the Prato della Valle. In the XIV century the land was purchased by the Scrovegni family who built their palace, which was torn down in the nineteenth century. The palace had been built to a plan that followed the layout of the arena. Today, the ruins of the Arena stand amidst a naturalistic type park with grottoes, waterfalls, ponds, and busts of famous figures, created on the basis of trends that became popular during the XIX century.

MUSEO CIVICO DEGLI EREMITANI

The building that houses the Museo Civico degli Eremitani.

To the left of the *church of the Eremitani* stand the ruins of the Convent of the same name, which, like the church itself, was struck by bombs during World War II. Today, the restored monastery houses the **Museo Civico degli Eremitani** to which all the municipal collections will gradually be brought.

For the time being, the museum contains the antique collections on the ground floor. The room dedicated to Venetic Culture opens the exhibit in a manner of speaking with some unique *funerary stele*. Then, there are objects that were placed in graves with the dead. The most significant of these are known as the *studded vases*, 88 superbly crafted pieces; then come the *zonated vases* with red and black bands and translucent decorations. The *lapidarium* contains artifacts from Roman Padua: busts, statues, votive offerings, funeral stele, sarcophagi, etc. Highlights from this grouping include a *bust of Augustus*, a *portrait of a woman*, with an elaborate, braided hairdo, a *Silenius* and the *Aedicula of theVolumni*, along with mosaics discovered during urban construction work. There are some very interesting items in the *Egyptian Collection* donated to the city by Giovan Battista Belzoni, one of the pioneers of modern Egyptology. The outstanding items here are a statue of the *goddess Sekmeth*, a sarcophagus in human shape, and a *Book of the Dead*, the parchment inscribed with prayers that were to accompany the deceased into the afterworld. Next come the items from the early Italian civilizations (Etruscan , Pre-Roman) and two big VII-VIII sailing vessels found in the vicinity of Padua. The early inhabitants of the area used them to sail up the rivers.

Giorgione, Leda and the Swan, Museo Civico degli Eremitani.

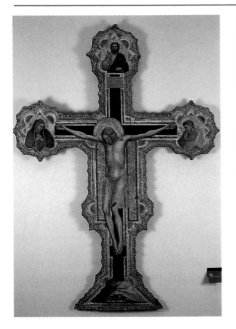

Other rooms in the museum contain Medieval art; the Renaissance bronzes include some works by Bartolommeo Ammannati; and finally there are some exhibits of nineteenth century paintings such as the *Bottacin Collection.*

Of the countless artworks in the Museum, a few exceptional items from the Medieval and Modern collections on the first floor deserve special mention. First, there is a thirteenth century plaster *Virgin and Child* by the Paduan sculptor Rinaldo Rinaldi; then a marble bas-relief by Canova portraying *Grateful Padua offering Gifts to Nicolò Antonio Giustiniani* and the *Repentant Magdalene*, a plastercast (probably original) by Canova as well. The artist had found several patrons among the wealthy citizens of Padua who admired his works from the start of his career.

The famous *Crucifix* by Giotto probably stood in the middle of the Arena Chapel so that even the fine decorations on the back could be admired. These paintings were done by pupils of Giotto's school. The custom in Medieval and Renaissance workshops was for the"master" to work on the main parts of the paintings, leaving the secondary or lateral parts to his disciples. There are many panels by Guariento that were originally part of the Chapel's ceiling which was dismembered in the eighteenth century during the Carrarera dominion, and finally, there is a *polyptych* (ex. n. 399) painted by Francesco Squarcione between 1449 and 1452.

Other noteworthy items are the *Descent of Jesus into Limbo* (ex n. 416) by Jacopo Bellini and the *Portrait of a Venetian Senator* by Giovanni Bellini (ex n. 43); a *Pastoral Scene* (ex n. 170) and *Leda and the Swan* (ex n. 162) probably by Giorgione; the *Birth of Adonis* (ex n. 50) and the *Myth of Erysichthon* (ex n. 56) which some have attributed to Titian, and then a *Virgin and Child with Saint Giovannino and Saint Sebastian* (ex n. 444) both signed by Marco Palmezzano.

The jewels and most of the paintings, in addition to the book collection were bequeathed by old, noble Paduan families; the exhibit is not yet complete since many items are still in storage.

CHAPEL OF THE ANNUNCIATION or SCROVEGNI or ARENA CHAPEL

Arena Chapel, exterior.

Opposite page: *Arena Chapel, interior.*

Rendering of the building that once housed the Arena Chapel.

From the museum we reach the area behind the Roman Arena and then the **Arena Chapel**.

When the Scrovegni palace was torn down, the *Chapel of the Annunciation* fortunately escaped destruction; it stood near the residential part of the complex and had been built by Enrico Scrovegni (1303) in memory of his father, Reginaldo, whom Dante had condemned to Hell (in the *Divine Comedy*) as being guilty of usury. The subdued façade, which had a balcony prior to the nineteenth century (there are still traces of it in the masonry), has pendent arches with three-light windows and a portal with a semi-circular lunette. On the southern wall are six single-light windows. The interior is characterized by a barrel-vaulted ceiling, an unusual shape for its era, a rectangular apse at the end and a polygonal apse with two single-light windows on the sides. The walls are decorated with one of the most important Medieval fresco cycles by Giotto who may have designed the building itself. With these frescoes the artist opened a new chapter in the representation of space in painting through the innovative relationship between the figures and the landscape that now, brilliantly and in a modern mode, went that crucial step beyond contemporary Byzantine rigidity or stiffness. The scenes all seem to have been immersed in live, human settings.

Giotto, Christ Enthroned With Angels, Arena Chapel.

Arena Chapel, entrance wall, with the Last Judgement.

Giotto, Paradise, Arena Chapel.

The frescoes are divided into three registers arranged on a base that recalls colored marble, alternating with panels containing monochrome allegories of the *Vices* and *Virtues*. There are thirty-eight frescoed panels with scenes from the *Life of the Virgin and Christ*. Most of them are based on the Apocrypha and date from 1305-06, that is the height of Giotto's artistic maturity, after he had completed the frescoes at Assisi.

On the wall opposite the entrance, in the "arch of triumph" above the doorway that leads to the small rectangular apse where the *Tomb of Enrico degli Scrovegni* is located, is a portrayal of *Christ Enthroned With Angels*, above the door is the *Last Judgement* and below, *Scrovegni Offering the Model of the Chapel to the Virgin*.

Giotto, The Inferno, Arena Chapel.

Giotto, The Patron, Enrico Scrovegni, offers a Model of the Chapel to the Virgin, Arena Chapel.

Giotto, Expulsion of Joachim from the Temple, Arena Chapel.

The actual narration of the cycle starts from the highest register on the right hand wall with *Scenes from the Life of the Virgin and Her Family*. The first picture is the *Expulsion of Joachim from the Temple* (Joachim was Mary's father); the architecture of the temple is more an allusion than an actual potrayal. Next comes *Joachim's Return to the Sheepfold* and the *Annunciation to Saint Anna* a scene in which Giotto, by showing a girl spinning in a corner, brought a touch of daily life and domesticity into a subject that was usually dealt with in a monumental manner. The artist's purpose was to emphasize divine intervention in daily life. The landscape, which also appears in other scenes, is painted with the massive force typical of the artist's style. Then come the *Annunciation to Joachim*; *Joachim's Dream*; *Anne and Joachim Meet in Jerusalem*. Here, the fusion of the two figures gives an explicit indication of the love each had for the other. The cycle continues on the same register, but on the opposite wall (to the left as we enter), with the *Birth of the Virgin*, and then the *Presentation of the Virgin in the Temple*; then, a few panels on the *Marriage of the Virgin*, and finally, on the opposite wall, *The Annunciation with the Angel* on the left, and the *Virgin* on the right of the entrance to the apse.

Giotto, Birth of the Virgin, Arena Chapel.

Giotto, The Marriage of the Virgin, Arena Chapel.

Giotto Annunciation, detail of the Angel (above left), and *detail of the Virgin* (above), *Arena Chapel.*

Giotto, Visitation, Arena Chapel.

Giotto, Adoration of the Magi, Arena Chapel.

Opposite page: *Giotto, Judas' Betrayal, detail, Arena Chapel.*

Giotto, The Flight into Egypt, Arena Chapel.

Giotto, Baptism of Christ, Arena Chapel.

The first panel in the middle register on the right wall, next to the apse shows Scenes from the Life of Christ, with the *Nativity*, the *Adoration of the Magi* and *The Presentation at the Temple*. In *The Flight into Egypt* there is a precise compositional relationship between the masses: the pyramid shaped mountain contains the figure of Mary who, in turn, forms a second pyramid-shape, holding the Infant Jesus.

Next comes the *Slaughter of the Innocents*. In the middle register on the left wall, near the entrance door are the paintings of *Jesus between the Doctors of the Law*, the *Baptism of Jesus* and the series of Christ's miracles: The *Wedding At Cana*; the *Raising of Lazarus*. In the first panel on the bottom near the apse on the right wall, is the *Last Supper* and *Judas' Betrayal* in which the figure of the Christ, enveloped in Judas' yellow robe seems to recall the image of a bird in the clutches of a predator while the faces, though physically close, remain distant.

In the third panel on the left starting from the entrancedoor is the *Lamentation*. The tendency here is to convey the desperation that extends even to nature itself, with that incision in the middle of the painting created by the diagonal line of the rock that crosses the scene, in addition to the writhing angels and the expressions on the faces of those who have seen the body. The desperation, however, is not lacking in majestic dignity, in the great balance between the volumes of the various figures. The next panel shows the *Resurrection* and finally, the *Ascension* and *Pentecost*, in which the critics say that the hand of Giotto's helpers is quite evident.

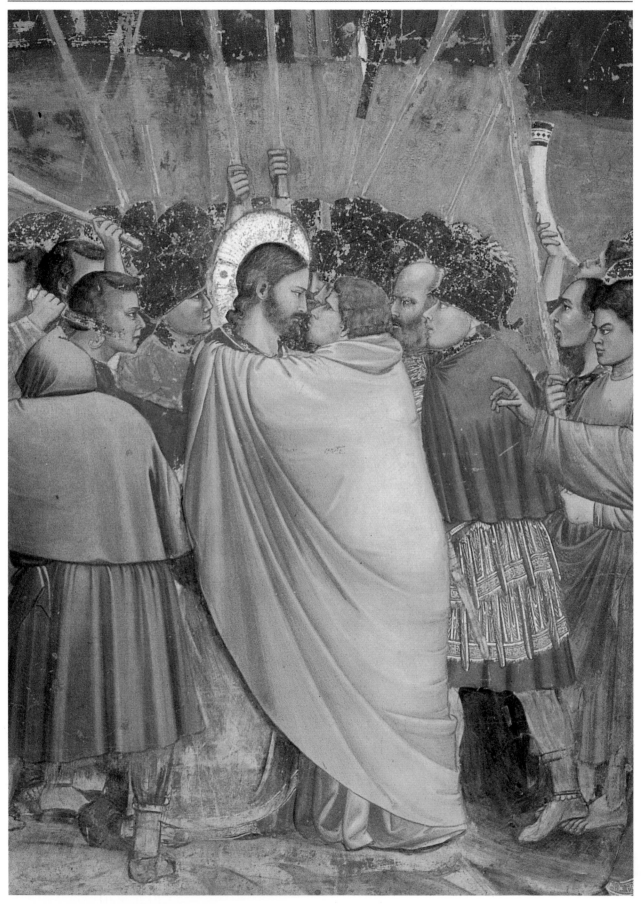

Giotto, (from the top), *The Wedding at Cana, Raising of Lazarus, Lamentation , The Resurrection, Arena Chapel.*

Giotto, Ascension, Arena Chapel.

INFIDELITAS

FIDES

Giotto, Allegory of the Vices (from the left), ***Envy and Faithlessness,*** *Arena Chapel.*

Giotto, Allegory of the Virtues (from the left), ***Faith and Temperance,*** *Arena Chapel.*

Church of the Eremitani,
façade (above);
southern door (below).
Opposite page: *interior*.

THE CHURCH OF THE EREMITANI

Built by the Hermits of St. Augustine in 1276 over an earlier building that dated from at least fifty years before, the church was initially a simple structure. Then the lateral chapels were gradually added over the centuries. The upper part of the façade is terracotta with pendent arches that follow the lines of the roof, a central rose window and four typical round windows. Below there is a marble structure with four, tall slim arches that allude to a portico which doesn't actually exist and which are curtained by, some even ancient, tombs. Perhaps it served as a model for Leon Battista Alberti's Tempio Malatestiano at Rimini. The arches, that were added later, obviously served to enhance and modernize the simple brick façade with a sort of precious decoration. On the southern wall is a *portal* built around 1442, with the *Months* by Niccolò Baroncelli, carved into the outermost lateral panels. Unfortunately, the poor condition of these carvings makes it impossible to fully comprehend their beauty and meaning.

Church of the Eremitani, Monument for the Tomb of Frederick William of Orange (bronze copy).

Inside the church, a large wooden ceiling, shaped like a ship's hull was built on the basis of the original from 1306. It too may have served as inspiration for Leon Battista Alberti's XV century work in Rimini (like the roof, destroyed by fire, of the Salone in the Palazzo della Ragione). The part of the choir with the chapels, destroyed by bombing raids in 1944, was rebuilt with much care dedicated to recovering the fragments of the ancient, destroyed frescoes. Along the single big nave, on the left wall is the *tomb of Jacopo da Carrara* and opposite, the *tomb of Ubertino da Carrara* dated 1350 and 1345, respectively by Andriolo de' Santi of Venice (the inscriptions on the stone are verses by Petrarch). On the left in the middle of the church wall is the *tomb of Marco Mantova-Benavides* (1546) by Bartolommeo Ammannati with statues in poses depicting vivid motion. In the first chapel on the right are fragments of frescoes by Giusto de' Menabuoi, and in the right transept, the *Ovetari or Mantegna Chapel*, which consists of a rectangular area preceded by an arch with a five-sided apse at the end. It was built between 1448 and 1457 by several artists including Mantegna, Vivarini, Ansuino da Forlì and others. The chapel was hit by bombs during the last World War. Only the frescoes of the *Assumption* (behind the altar) by Mantegna, the *Martyrdom of St. Christopher Beneath the Walls of Jerusalem* and the *Transport of the Saint's Body* (on the right wall) also by Mantegna were saved because they had been removed during the previous century. Attempts were made to recreate the *Martyrdom of St. James* by Mantegna from tiny fragments (it is now on the left wall).

These famous paintings are among the finest achievements of Renaissance art. One of the reasons being Mantegna's great skill in the use of illusions, perspective and masterly foreshortening.

Church of the Eremitani, Andriolo de' Santi, Tomb of Jacopo da Carrara (left); *Bartolomeo Ammannati, Tomb of Marco Mantova-Benavides* (right).

The *Assumption of the Virgin* was probably painted late in 1456. In the scene, enclosed by a vertical arch decorated with plants, the *Virgin* stands out against the dark background of the fresco, that is the night. She stands high, so that the viewer has a sensation of her rising to heaven, and even the mandorla surrounding the figure seems to emerge from the starry space within the arch. Then to accentuate the contrast, the painter highlighted the lower portion with the sky and below that, the figures of the Apostles who watch the miracle. In the *Martyrdom of St. James* (on the left) a severely deteriorated fresco, Mantegna used a series of illusionistic devices to bring the viewers into the painting as it were. It is sufficient to look at the cruel grimace on the face of the executioner who performs the gruesome decapitation. That the *Martyrdom of St. Christopher* (right) was one of the last works Mantegna painted here is borne out by various sources and even by the changes that the artist's concept of painting seems to have undergone. In the executioner, who seems to emanate cruelty, the artist now sought to convey more of an identification with evil, and hence a state of the soul. Criticized by Squarcione for not having adhered to the realityof his era (that is, "painting history"). Mantegna wanted to show that he knew how to use details and thus he dressed the figures in fifteenth century clothes and used friends of his as models for the faces of some of the characters. And finally, in the *Transport of the Saint's Body*, Mantegna aimed at creating an extreme unity with the other painting of St. Christopher, by using the same architectural setting for the episodes, with impressive, painted, marble and stone buildings, all placed in a paved square (on the wall of the royal palace there is a stone slab based on ancient Roman tombs to emphasize the Paduan liking for antiquities). The guards in the center of the painting dragging the enormous body of the Saint are yet another cruel element (perfectly in harmony with the painting of the Martyrdom), in which a miraculously deflected arrow, instead of striking Saint Christopher, hits the eye of King Danio di Licia the judge who had issued the death sentence.

Public slaughterhouse, entrance.

MANTOVA-BENAVIDES PALACE (or Venezze Palace)

This grandiose palace was built by Marco Mantova-Benavides. He perhaps wanted to have a square courtyard and a garden, connected by a triumphal arch flanking his residence. The palace has undergone many changes, even after the XVIII century restorations, and especially after the destruction caused by bombing raids during World War II. In fact, the interesting portions are the annexes and the courtyard, however an added building has totally upset the original proportions. There is a colossal, nine meter tall, *statue of Hercules*, with Ammannati's signature on the club. It is positioned eccentrically with respect to the axis so as not to block the view of the entrance to the palace and the arch. The statue, which was restored in 1994 stands on a pedestal decorated with the *Labors of Hercules* (Hydra, the River Acheloo and other mythical characters). The monumental entrance to the garden is graced by four, Doric columns. The rich decorations recall the treatise by Vignola who was a great friend of Ammannati. The niches contain statues of Jupiter and Apollo.

Public slaughterhouse, façade.

PUBLIC SLAUGHTERHOUSE
(now the Istituto d'Arte Pietro Selvatico)

In 1821 Giuseppe Jappelli who had recently studied the Greek temples of Paestum suggested a temple-like façade for the *public slaughterhouse*, perhaps to evoke images of ancient ritual sacrifices. The work was done using blocks of trachyte from the destroyed church of Sant'Agostino. In 1910, to transform the building into a school, the open courtyard with its Doric trabeated spans on one half, and curved wall on the other, was closed off by a reinforced concrete ceiling and windowed lantern. Notwithstanding its overall beauty, the complex is not at all in good condition today.

CHURCH OF SAN GAETANO

This church was designed by Vincenzo Scamozzi in 1581, and work was completed in 1586 as we can see from the inscription on the central door. The façade was probably inspired by ancient Roman ruins which Scamozzi had seen during a journey to Rome, and examples of buildings by Vignola. The lower part of the building is intensely chiaroscuro, whereas the upper part is absolutely linear with the exception of the thermal window in the middle. This creates a fine contrast especially in combining the two portions, which is achieved by protruding, brick pilaster strips made of plastered brick. The clear division between the two levels of the façade achieved by the protruding trabeation, the different architectural composition of the two parts and the diversities of the windows are the salient features of this important example of late Mannerist, nearly Baroque building.

The interior has an octagonal plan and is topped by a large dome. Each of the three lateral chapels is also domed. The marble decorations and dome frescoes by Guido Lodovico di Vernansal all date from the eighteenth century. Lodovico Vernansal also painted the *Flagellation* on the altar opposite the entrance. In the left chapel there is the *Presentation in the Temple* by Palma Giovane.

San Gaetano, the façade.

San Gaetano, Ruggero Bascapè, one of the statues in the niches next to the main altar (left); *the interior* (right).

CHURCH OF SANTA SOFIA

Santa Sofia, interior.

This, one of the oldest churches in Padua (IX century) was built by Venetian craftsmen. However, it was modified several times over the centuries. The current building 's façade leads us to believe that the upper part of the central portion with the two columns, the double light, the two windows and the arches date from the XII century; while the five blind arches of the central base and wings date from the XI century. This chronological division, is repeated inside the church as well, in spite of the overall "homogenization" that was achieved during various restorations with the cross vaults over the main nave (XI century columns decorated with acanthus leaves on the capitals alternate with pillars) and an external apse with niches dating from the IX century, and other, XII century Neobyzantine capitals.

In the apse there is a fragment of a *Virgin and Child* by Giovanni da Gaibana, in the Romanesque-Byzantine style of the XIII century. The *Pietà* on the second altar in the left nave is by Egidio da Wienerneustadt; this colored stone statue was carved in 1430 and is outstanding for the rich drapings of the Virgin's robes; some scholars have compared it to Baroque art for its intricacy.

Santa Sofia, façade.

Lando-Correr court.

MOCENIGO-QUERINI PALACE

Tradition maintains that a building designed by Andrea Palladio stood on this site, critics, however have other opinions. Either the house was built in 1558 to designs by Palladio who probably added a porticoed courtyard with niches and statues, while the façade was created by Agostino Righetti, or Palladio merely acted as a consultant without doing any major work on the building.

Mocenigo Palace, façade.

LANDO-CORRER COURT

The **Lando Court** is one of the few examples of what could be considered "low income housing" in the sixteenth century (there is a group of row houses attributed to Vignola in Bologna). It was built by Marco Lando, who left instructions on his death in 1513 that pàrt of his wealth be used to build a court with 12 dwellings and the church that closes it off, to create a "village" for the poor within the city. There is a garden behind each of the well restored houses. The church, however, is in urgent need of restorations.

CHURCH OF SAN FRANCESCO

San Francesco, façade.

This church, which was begun in 1416, was rebuilt during the XVI century. The work, did not affect the exterior with its Medieval façade, pendentives above and below the portico characterized by some Gothic arches and traces of frescoes (it is known that Squarcione worked on the church). Inside the naves are divided by columns and pillars while the ribs on the vaults are richly decorated. Highlights are the *Tomb of Bartolomeo Cavalcanti*, who died in 1562 (on the door of the right nave), and over the main door is a huge painting of the *Ascension* by Paolo Veronese (1575). In the right wing of the transept is a *Monument to Roccabonella*, a bronze dating from 1498 by Bartolomeo Bellano, a pupil of Dontaello (Pietro Roccabonella is portrayed in his study surrounded by books). On the left, is a fine relief of the *Virgin Enthroned* by Bellano and Briosco, and the altarpiece of the *Virgin and Child with Saints* by Paolo Pino (1565) which is also signed and dated. On the third altar in the left nave is an altarpiece with *St. Lawrence* by Padovanino.

San Francesco, interior.

San Francesco, Paolo Veronese, Ascension.

San Francesco, last altar in the right nave (right).

San Francesco, Bartolomeo Bellano, Monument to Roccabonella (left); *Filippo Parodi, Ecce Homo* (right).

The Pontecorvo Gate (left);
Cornaro Odeum (right).

PONTECORVO or LIVIANA GATE

This gate was built in 1517 in honor of the Captain General of the Venetian Republic, Bartolomeo d'Alviano who was responsible for the new, modern fortifications to most of the city's walls. Originally the gate was known as "Liviana" from the Captain's own name (Alviana), as we can still see from the inscription on top.

CORNARO LOGGIA and ODEUM

Alvise Cornaro, a great patron of the arts in the sixteenth century Venetian world, inherited a plot of land from a relative. Here he commissioned Giovan Mario Falconetto to build the *Loggia* (1524) that was to be used as a theater, and then perpendicularly to it an *Odeum* (1530-1538) taking the ancient name for a music room.

The **Loggia** has a portico with five arches, with masks on the keystone and decorations on the central one; inside there are frescoes by Falconetto. The statues of *Diana*, *Venus* and *Apollo* in the niches above have been attributed to Dentone or Zuan Padovano.

In the **Odeum** the relationships between the filled and empty spaces of the Loggia are totally inverted. On the ground floor are ediculae with reliefs, and the loggia is above. The interior is octagonal with niches and rectangular rooms each of which is richly decorated with frescoes and stuccoes, grotesques masks and mythological scenes. The entire complex was restored in 1994.

Equestrian Monument to Gattamelata *(piazza del Santo)*
Basilica di Sant'Antonio *(piazza del Santo)*
Oratory of San Giorgio *(piazza del Santo)*
Scuola di Sant'Antonio *(piazza del Santo)*
Former Civic Museum *(piazza del Santo)*

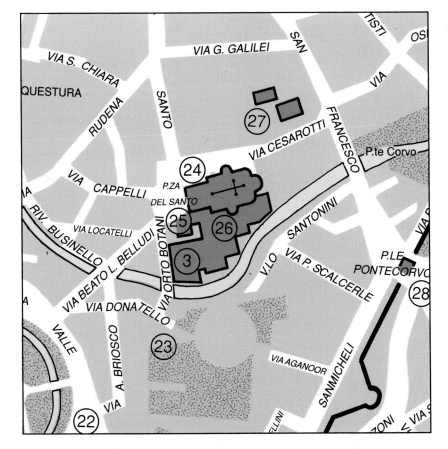

Equestrian Monument to Gattamelata

EQUESTRIAN MONUMENT TO GATTAMELATA

Donatello, equestrian monument to Erasmo da Narni, known as Gattamelata.

In the center of the square, in the area that was once the cemetery, and is now the Courtyard of the Basilica, stands the equestrian **monument to Erasmo da Narni, known as Gattamelata**, a knickname given because of his shrewdness. He fought for the Venetian Republic against the Visconti family of Milan and died in 1443. His widow and son commissioned Donatello, who was working on the church of the Saint (1443-1453 ca.) at the time, to build the bronze monument. It was the first of its kind in the Renaissance, and was based on ancient statuary. The solemnity of the composition, derived from relief carvings of Roman emperors, relays the tension in both the horse and rider, and continues in the trachyte and marble base with its rounded corners that Donatello modelled on ancient Roman funerary chapels. On each side is a door, one is open and the other partly closed, symbolizing the passage between life and death. In the attic, in line with the uprights, are two angels holding the coat of arms (the originals are in the cloisters of the Basilica museum). The monument was restored in 1994.

Aerial view of the Basilica di Sant'Antonio.

Detail of the Basilica seen from Via del Santo.

BASILICA DI SANT'ANTONIO (or Il Santo)

Brother Anthony, a Franciscan friar from Lisbon who was born around 1195, died in 1231 in the Santuario dell'Arcella (about one kilometer from what is now the Padua railroad sation). The monk had preached in Padua for two years before his death. In 1232, after he had been canonized by Pope Gregory, the citizens of Padua began building a new sanctuary on the site of the Romanesque *church of Mater Domini*; the sanctuary was to be dedicated to the new saint. Construction took many years. The main nave was built between 1256 and 1263, the other two were added later. It is difficult to accurately date the various parts of the church. The building was modified and partly destroyed many times, starting from the hurricane in 1394, and two fires in the XVI and XVIII centuries, respectively, so that major restorations were needed by the nineteenth century.

Basilica di Sant'Antonio (opposite page).

The distinguishing feature of the *outside* is a series of domes and slender bell towers that give the building a Byzantine and Islamic appearance. The domes are semispheric, the central one of the seven is a truncated cone and is 67 meters high. The two octagonal bell towers (finished in 1449) bear a strong resemblance to minarets.

Starting from the bottom, the *façade* has four large blind arches, over which there is a gallery with 17 small columns topped a pointed arch; then a marble balustrade, like the one on the gallery, and a rose window flanked by two double-lighted windows in the fronton on top. The *three bronze doors* to the church were made by Giuseppe Michieli in 1895 to designs by Camillo Boito. In the lunette of the small portal there is a 1940 copy of a fresco by Mantegna.

Basilica di Sant'Antonio, the north side.

Basilica di Sant'Antonio, façade.

Basilica di Sant'Antonio, detail of the bell towers and domes.

Basilica di Sant'Antonio (façade), Nicola Lochoff, Saints Anthony and Bernardino Worshipping the Christogram, fresco in the lunette above the main door (above); *Napoleone Martinuzzi, statue of Saint Anthony, in the niche above* (below).

Basilica di Sant'Antonio (façade), Camillo Boito, bronze door.

*Basilica di Sant'Antonio,
interior.*

The *interior* of the church is in the form of a Latin cross with three naves, the main one in the middle, and two smaller ones on the sides, separated by pillars. The naves continue beyond the transept and the lateral ones form a passage known as the ambulatory, to connect behind the main altar which is situated at the end of the main nave. Radial chapels open off the ambulatory, with the exception of the central and largest one which is round, they are all square-shaped.

It is this layout, used in conjunction with some special structural solutions that makes the Basilica resemble some French Gothic architecture, especially from the Perigord area. According to one hypothesis, the Basilica was built to architectural plans imported to Padua from beyond the Alps.

Starting from the right nave are the *altars of St. Bernardino* and *St. Carlo* (restored in 1994). The first chapel, known as the Gattamelata has the *Tomb of Gattamelata* on the left wall, and that of his son, *Giannantonio* from, the XV century on the right. In 1651 this chapel was dedicated to the *Blessed Sacrament* which is still worshipped here; the work was done by Lorenzo Bedogni and it remained unchanged until Ludovico Pogliaghi rearranged it entirely (1927-36) and had the *Souls* painted behind the altar.

Still in the right nave of the Basilica is the *Chapel of the Sacred Heart* (or St. Claire) that was built by Camillo Santuliana in 1624 (restored in 1994).

The transept is also a chapel and is dedicated to *St. James* and *St. Felix* (1372-1377); it contains a most interesting cycle of approximately 90 frescoes by Altichiero Altichieri of Verona and Iacopo Avanzo. They depict the *Life of St. James* and the *Crucifixion*. These frescoes are noteworthy for the many characters combined with a fine perception of depth, and the striking use of color.

In the *Council of the Crown* we can see many of the famous figures in fourteenth century Padua, including Petrarch. In fact, this cycle was an early example of a realistic "Gallery of Celebrities" (that was highly fashionable in the fifteenth century). The grand *organ*, dated 1895, is situated above this chapel.

The *main altar* at the end of the central nave is the last one built for the Basilica following a series of reconstructions. The first was a Gothic altar that was taken down to make room for the one by Donatello (1443-1450); next came the one built by Cesare Campagna and Cesare Franco (1579-1582), and finally the one we see today which is a not too successful attempt at rebuilding Donatello's altar by Camillo Boito (1895).

Basilica di Sant'Antonio, main altar.

Basilica di Sant'Antonio, Donatello, detail of the bronze crucifix on the main altar.

On the altar there is a large bronze *Crucifix* which is striking for the gaunt figure of Christ. This crucifix seems to have been the first commission Donatello received in Padua (1443-1444); originally it was not meant for its current setting. After Donatello's work on this part of the Basilica, the altar was quite different from the way it appears today. A high structure separated the area around the altar proper, which could be reached from the front, via a columned passage that opened towards the nave, much like the chapel in the transept. The altar, which was known "Anchona" in the fifteenth century was in this closed-off area so that it formed an isolated temple with columns and pillars mounted on bases, supporting a vaulted ceiling with lateral scrolls. Seven large statues of the *Virgin* and *Saints* stood beneath the temple ceiling. They still are here, but in different positions. On the walls of the altar (frontal and predella) were the *bronze panels* (1447-1448) by Donatello and his workshop. After Boito's restoration they were put back in their original settings.

Of these panels we must mention the *Miracles of Saint Anthony*: on the front of the altar is the *Miracle of the Amputated Foot*, or of the *Irascible Son* who had cut off his leg to punish himself after having kicked his mother; St. Anthony reattached his leg after he repented. Around the central scene, there is a square with steps that could be a theater. Leon Battista Alberti, Donatello's friend believed that "the place for entertainment is merely a square surrounded by steps".

The seond panel on the front of the altar depicts the *Miracle of the Miser's Heart*, set amongst Roman tombs outside the city, in accordance with the Paduan fashion for things Roman during the XV century. Next to the altar is a *candelabrum* made in 1515 by Andrea Briosco called "Il Riccio", the pedestal is by Francesco Cola.

On the other side are two more important panels by Donatello: *The Miracle of the Believing Donkey*, an episode that occurred in Rimini. The structure shown in Donatello's panel is very similar to Leon Battista Alberti's design for the Tempio Malatestian in Rimini, based on an architectural model that resembles the tomb of the ancestors in the temple. And finally, there is the panel of *Miracle of the Newborn Child* who testifies on behalf of his mother who had been unjustly accused.

Around the altar are other reliefs based on bronzes that decorated the original Donatello altar, such as the *Musical Angels*, a *Deposition* and a *Pietà*; on the walls around the altar are other works from Donatello's school that were made when the fourteenth century altar and railing were dismantled. These are bronze bas-reliefs portraying *Scenes from the Old Testament* (*Cain and Abel*; *The Egyptians Drowning in the Red Sea*; *The Golden Calf*; *Sampson in the Temple*, and others).

Before we reach the ambulatory, on the right nave, after the door leading to the cloisters is the *Sacristy* that contains a big marble reliquiary with wooden doors; the inlays were done by Da Lendinara to drawings by Francesco Squarcione in 1462 (not all are original, however).

From the sacristy we go to the *Chapter Room* in which there are fragments of fourteenth century frescoes.

Basilica di Sant'Antonio, Donatello, bronze crucifix on the main altar (opposite page).

**Basilica di Sant'Antonio,
Chapel of the Treasure.**

**Rainaldino, statue of the
Madonna Mora.**

Back inside the church, after going through the ambulatory that circles the choir, we come to the *radial chapels*. They were financed by different countries whose students were enrolled at the University of Padua. The third chapel with works by Martin Feuerstein is that of *Germany* (1907); next comes the Chapel of St. Stephen with frescoed scenes from the life of the Saint by Biagetti (1909). The next chapel is known as the chapel of the Treasure or of the Reliquaries, since the relics of St. Anthony were translated here in 1745. The chapel is entered via an anormous baroque portal; it was built on a circular plan in 1689 to designs by Parodi. It is typical of the era's taste for lavish use of colored marble and stuccowork. At the end there are three big arches containing the relics. They are surmounted by *Saint Anthony in Glory* by Parodi who also executed the other statues which are based on works by Bernini. The reliquaries inside the cabinets are fine examples of exquisite goldsmithing: the *Chin of Saint Anthony* dates from 1349, while the *Crystal Cross* and the *Saint's Tongue* were made in the XV century. On the left wall there are two caskets with the remains of the Saint which, according to tradition, date from the XIII century.

The next chapel is dedicated to *St. Stanislaus* and was frescoed in 1899; it is followed by the *Austrian Chapel*, decorated in 1932, and finally, the last one, the *Chapel of the Madonna Mora* built over the ruins of the ancient church of Santa Maria Domini. It gets its name from a dark complected statue of the *Virgin* made by Rainaldino in the XIV century. There are also several sarcophagi dating from the same period.

The *Chapel of the Blessed Luca Belludi* adjoins the chapel of the Madonna Mora. This chapel with its apsed walls was built in 1382 and dedicated to the Apostles Philip and James. The remains of Luca Belludi, a friend of St. Anthony were transferred here only in 1871. The sixty-eight frescoes were done by the Florentine artist Giusto de' Menabuoi the year the chapel was built. These paintings, which were restored in 1988 adorn the walls with scenes from the *Lives of Saints Philip and James* (on the left of the altar is an interesting portrayal of Medieval Padua with its towers), and a *Virgin and Child Enthroned.*

Basilica di Sant'Antonio, Chapel of the Blessed Luca Belludi frescoed by Giusto de'Menabuoi.

From the left side of the Chapel of the Madonna Mora, we go directly to the side of the transept that was transformed into the *Chapel of Saint Anthony* and where the Saint's tomb has been since 1310. After it was rebuilt (1500-1521) to plans by Andrea Briosco known as "Il Riccio", the tomb was placed in the green marble *sarcophagus* in the altar. There is a rood screen leading to it, adorned with *offerings* to the Saint. The screen, with steps, is preceded by five arches on columns and high pedestals creating a space between the burial site and the place of worship. There are five other arches on the back wall of the chapel. The perspective adds depth to the chapel. It is the work of Tiziano Aspetti who in 1593 rebuilt the Saint's tomb and placed nine reliefs by different artists from different periods between the chapel's arches. The fourth from the left portrays *Saint Anthony Reviving a Drowned Man,* by Jacopo Sansovino (1563); the fifth is *Saint Anthony Reviving His Sister's Son*, by Sansovino and Antonio Minello (1520-1534); the sixth and seventh, *Saint Anthony Helps the Miser Find his Heart*, and *Saint Anthony Reattaching the Foot*, by Tullio Lombardo (1524); the ninth, *The Miracle of the Newborn Child* was done by Antonio Lombardo (1505). The stuccoed ceiling is the work of Giovan Maria Falconetto and dates from 1533. It is the first example of this decorative technique in the region. The *angels* serving as bases for the candelabra on the altar are from the XVII and XVIII centuries.

Basilica di Sant'Antonio, votive offerings along the sides of the rood screen that leads to the altar of the Saint.

Basilica di Sant'Antonio, Chapel of the Blessed Sacrament (preceding page).

Basilica di Sant'Antonio, detail of the bas-reliefs in the Chapel of Saint Anthony.

Basilica di Sant'Antonio, Tomb of the Saint.

Basilica di Sant'Antonio, Stefano da Ferrara, Virgin of the Pillar (left); *Jacopo da Montagnana, Nativity and Saints, detail* (right).

Basilica di Sant'Antonio, Monument to Girolamo Micheli with a bronze bust of the deceased, by Francesco Segala.

As we leave the Chapel of Saint Anthony, the second tomb on the left nave is that of *Antonio Roselli* by Pietro Lombardo, dated 1464-67. Opposite the entrance to the basilica, atop a pillar is a *Virgin and Child*, known as the *Virgin of the Pillar*, which dates from the early XV century.

In addition to a pair of *holy water stoups* near the pillars in the central nave (the one on the right is by Tullio Lombardo, and the one on the left by Giovanni Minello or Tiziani Aspetti), is the *Monument to Alessandro Contarini*, the admiral who died in 1533. The sculpture is by Sanmicheli while the base with the pair of slaves and ships in perspective was executed by other artists: Graziosi, Vittoria and Danese Cattaneo. The *Monument to Pietro Bembo*, on the second pillar on the right was also designed by Sanmicheli and Cattaneo.

Back in the sacristy, before we go to the ambulatory on the right nave, a corridor leads to the *Cloisters* where there are tombs, coats of arms, etc. In the *Museo Antoniano* (which is currently being rearranged) is Andrea Mantegna's fresco of *Saints Anthony and Bernard Praying to the Christogram*. Originally this fresco, which dates from 1452, was in the lunette over the main door (the one there now is a copy), and it shows considerable signs of having been repainted.

In addition, the museum contains inlays taken from the cabinet in the Sacristy; and a panel of *Saint Bernardino,* by Giorgio Schiavone.

Basilica di Sant'Antonio,
Cloister of the Novitiate,
tomb (above); *the Cloister*
of the Novitiate (left).

Basilica di Sant'Antonio,
Cloister of the Novitiate,
loggia.

ORATORY OF SAN GIORGIO

Originally conceived as the funeral chapel for Raimondo Lupi da Soragna in 1379, the **oratory** (a simple room with a barrel vaulted ceiling like the Arena Chapel) is decorated with sculptures by Bonifacio Lupi and frescoes from 1384 by Altichiero Altichieri of Verona and his assistant Iacopo Avanzo which are still visible today in spite of much mishandling over the centuries. The *Tomb of Raimondo* which had been reduced to little more than fragments has been reassembled and placed on the left wall of the Oratory, while all the walls and ceiling are embellished by 22 large scenes and about one hundred paintings. On the front wall is The *Life of Christ*; over the altar is the *Crucifixion* and above the *Coronation of the Virgin*; at the entrance is the *Annunciation*, the *Flight into Egypt*, the *Presentation in the Temple*, so that the entire beginning and end of Christ's life on earth are portrayed.

On the walls are *Scenes from the Lives of Saints*: *Saint Catherine* above and *Saint Lucy* below.

On the left is the *Life of Saint George*, while the ceiling is decorated with *Saints* and *Angels*. This important fresco cycle fits into the context of Giottesque paintings, but the emphasis on color, as in Altichiero's works in the Chapel of Saint Anthony, is totally original. Furthermore, the narrative focuses on specific episodes, crowds, architecture, on portraits of the characters and filling the spaces. An excellent example is the *Beheading of Saint George* where the emptiness created by a stark depiction of the hill sloping above the characters is filled by the soldiers' lances that crowd into this space.

SCUOLA DI SANT'ANTONIO

The confraternity of Saint Anthony was founded immediately after his death in 1231; but the **Scuola** as it stands today was only built in 1427. Originally it was a chapel and became the *Confraternity's Meeting Place* in 1504. The façade was modified in 1732 when it was embellished with statues of **Saints** by Bonazza and his school. Inside the ground floor church, on the high altar is a Paduan canvas portraying the *Virgin and Child and Saints Benedict and Jerome*.

The room above is covered with frescoes and three oil paintings that highlight the colors on the walls. It is an important chapter in sixteenth century Venetian painting because of the works by Titian and his followers (1511). In these episodes of the *Miracles of Saint Anthony*, Titian reveals his great talent for tonality, that is broad areas of color that bring the scenes to life. Within the cycle we must point out the portions that have been attributed to the master himself: the second, from the right, in which the Saint performed the *Miracle of the Newborn Child*; the twelfth scene with *Miracle of the Jealous Husband*, and the next one depicting the *Miracle of the Irascible Son*.

Scuola del Santo, façade (opposite page).

MONASTERY OF THE EREMITANI (Civic Museum)

In 1871 the collections in some of the rooms of the Palazzo Comunale were moved to that wing of the Monastery which is now known as the "**Museo Civico**". Eugenio Maestri was given the task of arranging the new rooms, the work was completed by the architect Camillo Boito who added the *big door* and *grand staircase*. The staircase has been severely criticized because, like the rest of the building, Boito wanted to decorate it with stucco-work and cornices that combined several styles in the eclectic-historicist late nineteenth century manner. Today, due to a lack of space, the collections are exhibited in the Museo degli Eremitani (where they are displayed alternately due to space problems). This building on the Piazza del Santo is used for temporary exhibits. In the entrance lobby there is a statue by the young Antonio Canova (1778) of *Alvise Vallaresso* portrayed as Aesculapius.

Monastery of the Eremitani, site of the Civic Museum

Palazzina Tron *(via dell'Orto Botanico)*
Botanical Gardens *(via dell'Orto Botanico)*
Prato della Valle
Basilica of Santa Giustina *(Prato della Valle)*
Palazzo Zacco *(Prato della Valle)*
Loggia Amulea *(Prato della Valle)*
Palazzo Broccadello and **Palazzina Molin**
(Corso Vittorio Emanuele II)
Church of Santa Croce
(Corso Vittorio Emanuele/piazzale Santa Croce)
Porta Santa Croce *(piazzale Santa Croce)*

Third Itinerary

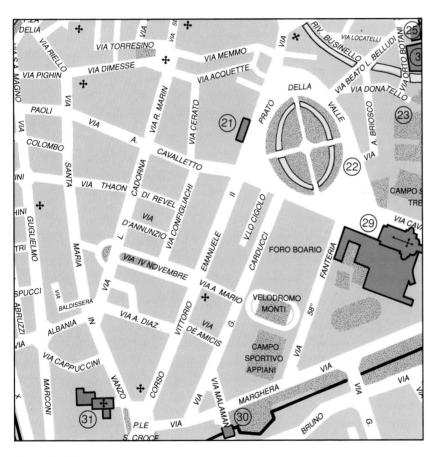

Palazzina Tron

Palazzina Tron, façade.

Opposite page, from the top:
*fountain with the statues of
the four seasons and
Solomon located near the
eastern door* and *a
sub-fossil oak trunk dating
from approximately the III
century B.C*

*Botanical Garden,
ancient sequoia.*

PALAZZINA TRON

This seventeenth century palace has been attributed to the Venetian architect Baldassare Longhena. The central part of the façade features flattened pillars right up against the wall (pilaster strips) on all three floors. On the ground floor these strips consist of smooth stone blocks, while on the upper floors they are actually plaster. The building is topped by a pitched marble roof (fronton); ends of the beams (mutules) protrude considerably creating a decorative chiaroscuro effect typical of Longhena's work.

BOTANICAL GARDENS

Built to designs by Andrea Moroni, the **Botanical Gardens**, one of the first in Europe was established in 1545, even if an original nucleus seems to have been in existence as early as 1533. Except for the outside wall and great portal that was initially made of big, rough stone blocks, (and which were replaced early in the eighteenth century) the central part of the garden is still the original. It is surrounded by a wall with four openings and a balustrade. Behind the area bounded by the wall are the medicinal and rare plants; outside are the arboretum and the conservatory with a plant, the *Vitex Agnus Castus*, that dates from 1550 (restorations were done in 1994).

PRATO DELLA VALLE

Prato della Valle, detail.

In the Middle Ages this area was an unhealthy swamp that was formed after the fall of the Roman Empire, it had been the site of the *Zairo theater*. The foundations of that great building were discovered in 1775 when the square was rebuilt to the way it looks today. The idea of reclaiming the land after various attempts starting from the XIV century can be attributed to Andrea Memmo, Special Superintendent of the Republic. He wanted to a create an area to revitalize the city, with shops, a fairgrounds, and theatrical performances capable of attracting patrons. A student of Carlo Lodoli and architectural writer, Memmo wanted an eliptical piazza with a central canal that could receive and drain water via underground ducts, with an island in the middle that would be linked to the rest of the piazza by four bridges. A tree-lined avenue runs all around; obelisks positioned at two of the bridges mark the minor axis of the island; eighty statues on pedestals commemorate illustrious figures from Padua's past. The *statue of Poleni*, physicist and mathematician was done by the young Canova. In the middle of the island there is a relatively new fountain, and on the avenues, stone vases are mounted on pedestals. The aim is to create pleasant stopping places or, elements which can enliven the avenue with picturesque, scenic effects. Some authors have connected this avenue with initiation rites inspired by the Masonic ideals shared by Andrea Memmo and Domenico Cerato, the architect who built the Prato.

**Prato della Valle,
aerial view.**

Prato della Valle, detail of the shore with statues and bridges.

Prato della Valle, the fountain in the middle of Memmia Island.

Prato della Valle at night.

Basilica of Santa Giustina, façade (above); *marble gryphon of Verona in the basilica courtyard* (below).

BASILICA OF SANTA GIUSTINA

Justina was martyred by the Emperor Maximianus because of her religion. The church stands on the site of the old cemetery where the saint's body had been laid. The place, which became a burial site for Christians, has yielded up the *tomb of Saint Prosdocimus*, the oldest Christian structure found in Padua to date. When the Longobards besieged the city, they spared this place of worship which stood until 1117 when it was destroyed by a terrible earthquake. In 1498 a decision was made to build a new basilica. Andrea Moroni was chief architect from 1532 to 1560, but his plans were never completed, as we can see from the still unfinished façade.

The large *interior* is divided into three naves by huge pillars and lateral chapels according to a "modern" basilica plan which, starting from the Basilica of San Lorenzo in Florence (mid-fifteenth century) became almost a standard throughout Italy. The end portion of the choir with circular chapels and domes has the same Eastern flair, albeit in smaller size, of the Basilica di Sant'Antonio.

In the fifth chapel on the right, is a painting signed by Palma il Giovane (1618) portraying *Saint Benedict with Saint Mauro and Saint Placido;* the adjacent chapels contain other works from the XVII century. From the right transept via a corridor on the left we come to the *Tomb of Saint Prosdocimus* (V century), nearby is an ancient altar made of Greek marble and an inscription commemorating the construction of the early Basilica. Inside the church again, we see a XV century wooden *Crucifix* that is remarkable for the anatomy of the body and facial expression. To the right, before we reach the presbytry is a chapel with the *Pietà* by Parodi (1689), an excellent example of Baroque sculpture as evident in the accentuated positions of the bodies of the *Christ* and the *Virgin.* In the presbytry is a fine, carved wooden *choir* with stalls dated 1467-77 and then the *walnut great choir,* (1558-1566) carved and inlaid with scenes from the Old and New Testaments. At the back of the choir is the altarpiece signed by Paolo Veronese, the *Martyrdom of Saint Justina* (1575), and in the transept the *Tomb of Saint Luke,* dated 1316, of the Pisan school.

Preceding page: ***Basilica of Santa Giustina, interior*** (above) ; ***the first two chapels on the left nave*** (below, left); ***Filippo Parodi, Pietà*** (below, right).

Basilica of Santa Giustina, Well of the Martyrs.

Basilica of Santa Giustina, Pietro Damini, the Blessed Giacoma Discovers the Well of the Martyrs, canvas on an altar in the Corridor of the Martyrs.

Amulea Loggia, façade.

PALAZZO ZACCO

Amulea Loggia, one of the bridges leading to the Prato della Valle.

This palace, designed by Andrea Moroni has a façade with a nine-arcade portico; the arches vary in size, the three central ones are the smallest and they are supported on pillars of false ashlar; the central portion, on the first storey has three, big arched windows. A cornice divides the first storey from the mezzanine (where the servants were quartered) which is characterized by simple, rectangular windows. Completed between 1555 and 1567, the façade is decorated with two finely made coats of arms in Istrian stone.

AMULEA LOGGIA

This **loggia** gets its name from Cardinal Marco Antonio da Mula or Amuleo who had established a school in a small building here; it was destroyed in 1822. The loggia we see today, after the XIX century fire that struck the area, was rebuilt in the Neo-Gothic style in red and white on ten octagonal pillars by Maestri between 1859 and 1861. This is yet another example of nineteenth century esthetic trends in Padua that drew heavily from the French fashion for Neo-Medieval *revivals* (the façade was restored in 1994).

PALAZZO BROCCADELLO and PALAZZINA MOLIN

The façade of **Palazzo Broccadello** (n.175) is in the Venetian Gothic style: although the date of construction is unknown, it would seem to be a nineteenth century remake. In fact, the building that dates from the fifteenth century was rebuilt and modified many times over the years. The façade may originally have been decorated with frescoes; today we can admire the architectural details, such as the windows framed by elegant, narrow spiral columns.

Palazzina Molin (n.142) situated in a paved courtyard is believed to have been designed by Falconetto or another predecessor of Palladio. There are some sources that attribute it to Andrea della Valle or even Vincenzo Scamozzi who worked for the Molin family on a villa at the gates of the city. The façade of the palace is characterized by three full arches closed on the sides by pilaster strips that rise uninterruptedly from the ground floor to the roof to form what is known as a "giant order". The second floor does not have real windows as on the first floor, but rather round oculi. Above there is a high, decorated cornice that circles the entire façade. It is likely that there was supposed to have been a big, triangular roof (fronton) as on temples, however, it was never built.

Palazzo Broccadello, two views of the façade.

CHURCH OF SANTA CROCE

This church was built in the XVI century, and was rebuilt in the XVIII; the central part of the façade is marked by two lateral columns and the large central fronton with its rich decorations. The *interior* consists of single nave and balconied windows that face inside. The windows aroused much criticism when they were built as they were considered more appropriate for a theater rather than a house of worship. On the ceiling are paintings depicting the *Triumph of the Cross*, on the main altar there are two *Angels* in Carrara marble carved by Antonio Bonazza in 1733. In the *Parish Hall*, the former *Oratory of the Confraternità del SS. Redentore* (confraternity of the Redeemer), all the walls were frescoed by Domenica Campagnoli and Gerolamo del Santo in 1537 even if restorations over the centuries make it difficult to attribute specific parts with precision.

Santa Croce, façade.

PORTA SANTA CROCE

This gate, built in 1527 is surmounted by statues of *Saint Prosdocimus* and *Saint Jerome*.

Porta Santa Croce.

Church of Santa Maria del Torresino
(via Marin/via Memmo/ via del Seminario)
Seminary and **Church of Santa Maria in Vanzo** *(via del Seminario)*
Astronomical Observatory *(via Osservatorio Astronomico)*
Palazzo Candi and **Collegio Barbarigo** *(via dei Rogati)*
Church of Santa Maria dei Servi *(via Roma)*
Bank of Italy Building *(via Roma)*
Tomb of Antenore and **Monumento to Lovato de' Lovati**
(piazza Antenore)
Palazzo Romanin-Jacur and **Palazzo Sala** *(piazza Antenore)*
University *(via VIII Febbraio)*
Church of San Canziano
Caffè Pedrocchi *(piazzetta Pedrocchi/piazza Cavour)*

Fourth Itinerary

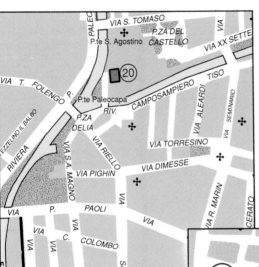

Santa Maria del Torresino

Santa Maria del Torresino, lateral view.

Santa Maria del Torresino, façade.

Santa Maria del Torresino, apse.

CHURCH OF SANTA MARIA DEL TORRESINO
or DEL PIANTO

This church is commonly called "**del Torresino**" because of the tower that crowns the dome, and which seems to have been derived from a tower that once stood on the ancient city walls. Inside the church there is a miraculous effigy of *Our Lady of Sorrow* that began to work miracles in the mid-XV century. The church, as we see it today, was redesigned by Gerolamo Frigimelo, and was completed in 1726 with a late Baroque façade in the typical style of the period. Excellent examples of this style can be seen in the corners which are not all emphasized as usual. In fact, the architect wanted to create an impression of movement. The columns on the façade are flanked by others which by combining their cylindrical shape with those of the first and outer row, more or less camouflage the lines of the church's corner. This is one of the optical tricks that were so fashionable during the Baroque and late Baroque periods.

The plan of the building's *interior* is circular with a large rectangular vestibule (at the entrace) and three apsidial chapels. In the middle, above the main altar is a large dome supported by columns. The statues in the niches, by Bonazza, portray the virtues (*Patience, Prudence, Chastity*, etc.) and date from the mid-XVII century. They are truly fine pieces of sculpture, with cleanly finished surfaces that reflect light in an extraordinary manner.

The *Dead Christ in the Arms of the Virgin* was done by Sartori in1940 and it stands between other statues (*Saint John* and *Mary Magdalene*) by Bonazza.

SEMINARY and CHURCH OF SANTA MARIA IN VANZO

This building, erected by Cardinal Barbarigo in 1671, was enlarged in 1756 by the future Pope Clement XIII. Inside there is a *Museum* and an important *Library* containing valuable books, incunabulae, a letter by Petrarch and manuscripts by Galileo.

On the left, still in the Seminary complex, is the **church of Santa Maria in Vanzo**, a building with a very plain façade. It was built in 1436 and was expanded in 1525. However, most of the original, Gothic proportions were left intact. The entrance portal dates from the fifteenth century. The single nave inside is flanked by small arches that support the galleries and nine altars, where we can admire sixteenth century Flemish (the first painting on the left) and Venetian artworks. One of the early paintings by Domenico Campagnola is on the front of the old rood screen which was moved to the façade wall (1945 - 46) where it still stands from the its original position in the middle of the nave; the wooden *Crucifix* dates from the fifteenth century.

ASTRONOMICAL OBSERVATORY

Known as "**La Specola**" the observatory was established in a Medieval tower that dates from the XIII century, which was built over an even older high Medieval structure. It became an **Observatory** in 1761 when the building was remodelled: large ashlar framed windows, the terrace and the highest part of the tower were added at that time.

Torlonga or Specola, the main tower of the castle that belonged to Ezzelino III da Romano, now headquarters of the Astronomical Observatory.

PALAZZO CANDI and THE COLLEGIO GREGORIANO BARBARIGO (formerly Casa Genova)

Both of these palaces in Via Rogati were built between the fifteenth and sixteenth centuries.

Palazzo Candi (n.17) has an interesting first floor façade; where single- and double- and quadruple windows alternate. The double window has a central pilaster, while the three columns embellish the quadruple one. All the openings are arched and the surrounding masonry consists of elements of the same size which are known as isodomons. On the ground floor the stones are laid diagonally as in a Roman *opus reticulatum*. This building, that dates from the late XV/-early XVI century has been attributed to Lorenza da Bologna.

The **Casa Genova** (nos. 30-34) also has alternating double (on the wings) and triple (with rounded-headed arches) on the central portion windows. Once again, the flat pilaster strips break up the façade vertically, while the stone arches as in Palazzo Candi consist of blocks that are all the same size.

Andrea Palladio was born in house number 8 on this same street.

Palazzo Candi.

Collegio Gregoriano Barbarigo seen from the loggia.

Santa Maria dei Servi,
Jacopo da Montagnana,
Pietà.

Santa Maria dei Servi,
interior.

Santa Maria dei Servi,
wooden Crucifix (XV cent.).

CHURCH OF SANTA MARIA DEI SERVI

This church was built in 1372 with a single nave, a sloping façade and arches known as "Lombard". In the upper coping there is a portico supported by red marble columns on one side (originally these columns stood in the old Chapel of Sant'Antonio). The portico was added by Bartolomeo Campolongo in 1511. In 1926 the church was in disastrous conditions, the existing wooden ceiling was built at that time, and the walls were reinforced.

The *interior* of the church is quite remarkable. On the left is a fifteenth century *Pietà* attributed to Jacopo da Montagnana. In the Chapel of the Crucifix there is a mid-fifteenth century *wooden crucifix* from Donatello's school, emphasizing the importance of the Master's cultural contribution to the Padua area. And finally, there is the *Altar of Our Lady of Sorrow* by Giovanni Bonazza (dated between 1710 and 1730).

BANK OF ITALY BUILDING

The building that houses the **Banca d'Italia** (or Bank of Italy) is an extremely modern structure designed by Giuseppe and Alberto Samonà in the late 'sixties (1968-74). It bears a close relationship to the Medieval (or nineteenth century neo-Medieval) architecture in Padua with the big pillars on the façade that are finished at the top to resemble the crenellations on a castle. The portico with its lowered arches is not a public passageway like most porticoes, but rather a "private" stopping place for people coming to the bank.

Bank of Italy Building.

TOMB OF ANTENORE and MONUMENT TO LOVATO DE' LOVATI

The skeleton of a Hungarian soldier, discovered in 1274, was considered to be that of Antenore; the mythical founder of Padua. This tomb, dedicated to him was constructed in 1283. Sheltered by an aedcula supported by two columns and two pillars is the simple sarcophagus which in turn, rests on four low colums, with only four lateral elements acroteria emerging on top. The section of wall that protrudes from the aedicula was part of the now demolished church of San Lorenzo against which the tomb stood until the 'thirties.
The other tomb near that of Antenore is that of the prehumanist, Lovato de' Lovati. It is known that he wanted his tomb to be a sort of trunk, decorated with lions on top and supported by four slim columns. This sarcophagus, placed in front of an important house of worship as the church of San Lorenzo was, brings to mind the Tombs of the Glossatori in Bologna, other great men considered symbols and cultural leaders of their city.

Tomb of Antenore, Monument to Lovato de'Lovati.

Palazzo Sala.

PALAZZO ROMANINI JACUR and PALAZZO SALA

Palazzo Romanin Jacur (n.9) was the object of nineteenth century restorations that aimed at recreating a Venetian building with lobated single and double-lighted windows in line with the then dominant historistic and pictorial trends. This building shares several features, therefore, with the Broccadello building. They may have been done by the same hand, or at least in pursuit of a common esthetic goal.
Palazzo Sala (n.11) on the other hand, which was built in 1507, reveals the popularity of diamond-point decorations in the Padua area. It was first used on the Palazzo dei Diamanti in Ferrara and then here, by the architect Lorenzo da Bologna, on the pillars and arched lintels of the windows.

THE UNIVERSITY or PALAZZO DEL BO

Although the first students and professors from Bologna moved to Padua in 1222, the two Schools of the "jurists" and of the "artists" were officially authorized in 1399. The two universities had separate premises until 1522. Reconstruction lasted until 1601 when the building acquired on its current form. It was home to the university until 1922 when G. Fondelli redesigned the structure so that it would take up the entire city block. The oldest wing has a *Courtyard* with a two-tiered loggia, Doric on the ground floor and Ionic above, in accordance with what was considered an overlapping of architectural orders. The walls of the building that was designed by Andrea Moroni is decorated with the coats of arms of rectors and students according to a custom that we can also see in the Palazzo dell'Archiginnasio of Bologna.

Palazzo del Bo, façade.

Palazzo del Bo, XVI century inside courtyard designed by Andrea Moroni.

Palazzo del Bo, Bernardo Tabacco's Monument to Elena Lucrezia Cornaro Piscopia, the world's first woman university graduate.

Palazzo del Bo (Entrance Hall of the Heroes), Artura Martini Palinuro.

Palazzo del Bo, the Chair of Galileo Galilei.

Palazzo del Bo, the old archives.

From the upper loggia we reach the *School of Medicine*, where the wall frescoes were done by Achille Funi (1942); then the *Anatomy Theater* with its elliptical plan and conical cross-section; in the center there is a dissecting table. This Theater, designed in 1594 was the first of its kind anywhere. Even the premises of the *Faculty of Arts* and *Philosophy, Law* and *Science* were also decorated by contemporary artists including Gino Severini. These university buildings actually host an unique anthology of twentieth century murals. In the *Aula Magna Vecchia* or *Great Hall* is the chair that is believed to have been Galileo's, whereas the current Great Hall was rebuilt by Giò Ponti in 1942; the same architect also worked on the *Rector's Office* (where there are works by De Pisis and Manzù) and on the *Grand Staircase* in the *Rectorate*.

Preceding page: Palazzo del Bo, Anatomy Theater (above); *Great Hall* (below).

San Canziano, interior.

San Canziano, façade.

CHURCH OF SAN CANZIANO

The **church of San Canziano** dates from the XI century, and was probably built over an earlier structure that collapsed during the earthquake that struck Padua around that time. The church was completely rebuilt in 1617 (masonry and decorations from the old building were brought to light during the most recent restorations). The *façade* is designed like a triumphal arch, with two semi-columns on a high pedastel; it is so elegant that some critics have attributed it to a student of Palladio. The façade is also embellished with a fresco (only little remains, unfortunately) by Ludovico de Vernansal, while statues by Bonazza stand in the niches.
Inside, on the high altar is a *Virgin and Saints* by Padovanino and early sixteenth century terracottas by Andrea Briosco. On the left altar is a terracotta statue of the *Dead Christ,* by Riccio (1503), flanked by the *Miracle of the Miser,* by P.Damini and the *Procession of San Carlo Barromeo,* by Bissoni.

CAFFÉ PEDROCCHI

This caffé was named after its founder, Antonio Pedrocchi. The building as it stands today, was completed by Giuseppe Jappelli in 1826. Since it was built on an unevenly shaped site, the architect solved this problem by dividing it into three sections for the three areas of business: the coffeehouse proper, the warehouse, and a smaller shop area with three façades. The problem of space distribution and coordination was solved by Jappelli who built two low loggias on columns to create a U-shaped courtyard (over which rises a loggia with Corinthian columns). Corinthian pilaster strips also adorn the left side façade while the narrow south side has a single Doric loggia. In 1838 Jappelli designed by the Neogothic part known as *Pedrocchino*, which proved his skill in all historic styles. The restoration work done in 1959 led to the opening of the gallery and three lateral doors.

Caffè Pedrocchi, outside.

Caffè Pedrocchi at night.

Caffè Pedrocchi, Sala Bianca
(White Room).

Inside, the eclectic tastes of Jappelli and the scuptors who worked with him (like Gradenigo) were elaborately developed in the differently decorated rooms. The *Sala Bianca* (or White Room) and the *Sala Rossa* (Red Room) are decorated with Ionic columns, and the *Sala Greca* (Greek Room) with Greek decorative designs. The *Saletta Etrusca* (Etruscan Room), the *Sala Rinascimentale* (Renaissance Room), the *Sala Ercolana*, the *Sala Egizia* (which may have been inspired by Jappelli's friend, Belzoni) and the *Gabinetto Moresco* are all quite obvious examples of the infinite possibilities that the nineteenth century offered to those artists who loved to move freely in time and space to seek their inspiration.

Municipal Government Buildings *(via VIII Febbraio/ via Moroni/ via Oberdan/ piazza delle Frutta/ piazza delle Erbe)*

Palazzo della Ragione

Loggia della Gran Guardia *(piazza dell'Unità d'Italia o dei Signori)*

Palazzo del Capitanio and **Arco dell'Orologio** *(piazza dei Signori)*

Corte Capitaniato, Loggia del Capitanio and **Liviano** *(via dell'Accademia)*

Loggia Carrarese *(via dell'Accademia)*

Arco Vallaresso *(Corte Capitaniato/ Corte Vallaresso/ piazza Duomo)*

Monte di Pietà *(piazza Duomo)*

Cathedral and **Baptistry** *(piazza Duomo)*

Oratory of the Colombini and **Palazzo Papafava** *(via dei Papafava/ via Barbarigo/ via Marsala)*

Bishop's Palace *(via Vescovado/ piazza Duomo)*

Palazzo degli Specchi *(via Vescovado)*

Porta San Giovanni *(Porta San Giovanni/ via Euganea)*

Teatro Verdi *(via Verdi/ piazza San Nicolò)*

Church of San Nicolò

Church of Santa Lucia and **Oratory of San Rocco**

Church and **School of Santa Maria del Carmine** *(piazza Petrarca)*

Fifth Itinerary

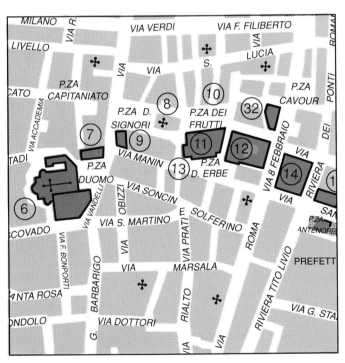

MUNICIPAL GOVERNMENT BUILDINGS

The area of the municipal government buildings, that is where the city hall is located, comprises three interconnected buildings: *Palazzo degli Anziani*, *Torre degli Anziani* and *Palazzo del Consiglio*, all of which date back to the comune period.

Palazzo degli Anziani faces onto Via Oberdan; it was built in 1285, and the large, groundfloor portico is typical of Medieval public buildings. The pillars, arranged assymmetrically are made of Istrian stone and support cross vaults. The third story was added in the sixteenth century, and the original double-lighted windows on the upper floors were replaced with rectangular ones in 1526. Only in the nineteen thirties, in keeping with the trend for restoring monuments were the original double-lighted windows replaced, and the masonry exposed. On the front of the building are the arms of the city and the Podestà.

Palazzo del Podestà (or city hall) faced onto Piazza della Erbe ever since the orignal building was completely reconstructed by Andrea Moroni, Superintendent of the palace from 1539 to 1560. The sixteenth century style is clearly visible in the groundfloor architecture, with roundedhead-ed arches on rusticated ashlar pillars. Above, the piano nobile is separat-ed from the groundfloor by a balustrade and tall windows with rounded arches. The windows are on a rusticated stone wall, with pilaster strips that rise as high as the roof and encompass the openings on the mezza-nine: an order of giant pilaster strips embraces two stories. The arms of the Barbaro family decorate the walls of the piano nobile.

Palazzo degli Anziani.

Palazzo del Podestà (left); *nighttime view of Palazzo Comunale* (right).

Piazza della Frutta.

Piazza della Frutta, loggia.

Piazza della Frutta, relief sculpture on one of the doors of the loggia.

Torre del Comune.

The **Torre degli Anziani** (or del Comune) was originally a private, nearly windowless tower. Double-lighted windows were added in the XVI centery and the tower was raised in 1620 by the addition of an octagonal lantern and a segmented dome. During the historic restorations of the 'thirties, the dome and lantern were eliminated to recreate the Medieval appearance according to the romantic tastes that prevailed early in this century. The **Palazzo del Consiglio** (which is also known as Palazzo degli Anziani) stands in Piazza della Frutta; it was built in 1283. On the ground floor there is a portico of Istrian stone, like the Palazzo degli Anziani; two Greek marble columns with Paleochristian capitals dating from the XI and XII century were reused, and finally, the arches here, too are roundheaded. At the ends, two large avant-corps frame the rest of the façade which is broken horizontally by pendentives that in turn, support the windowsills. In 1774 the original groundfloor arcades were all occupied by permanent shops.

Piazza delle Erbe, relief sculpture on a door inside the loggia.

Piazza delle Erbe.

Piazza delle Erbe, loggia.

Piazza delle Erbe, relief sculpture on a door inside the loggia.

Palazzo della Ragione, exterior.

PALAZZO DELLA RAGIONE known as IL SALONE

This palace was built between 1218-19, according to the municipal plans to house shops on the groundfloor, municipal offices and stores on the mezzanine, and the courts on the upper floor. The palace is basically a rhombus, oriented so that the sun's rays shining through the upper storey windows strike the Zodiac sign for the current month. This is just one proof of the enormous, painstaking work that went into the design of the building.

On the ground floor, the arches were "shielded" by the spans which form a sort of exterior portico. Shops were housed in the arches which, at the ends are broken by four monumental staircases that lead to the loggias from which one can reach the *monumental Salone* on the piano nobile. These large rooms were reconstructed between 1306-09 by Fra' Giovanni degli Eremitani who built the huge ceiling in the shape of an overturned ship's hull, which is supported inside by iron chains. This is also when Giotto and his followers (1315-17) frescoed the walls of the Salone with a cycle inspired by Pietro d'Abano, and thus they associated Medieval cosmology and astrology with the practice of justice in the rooms that house the Court of Padua.

Palazzo della Ragione, detail of the outside loggia.

Palazzo della Ragione, Il Salone, detail of the ceiling shaped like an overturned boat (above, left); ***detail of the frescoes in the Salone*** (above); ***the Salone*** (top, right).

Palazzo della Ragione, Il Salone, the "pietra del vituperio".

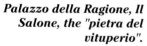

In 1420 a fire destroyed the roof and damaged the frescoes as well. A new roof was built, with trusses supported by four large leather-covered columns. The paintings were redone once by Nicolò Moretto and then in 1770 by Francesco Zannoni. The scenes are divided in two registers: the first below depicts *Allegories of the Virtues* (by Giusto de' Menabuoi, dated approximately 1375), coats of arms, and *Saints*. The second, and higher register is divided into 333 scenes arranged in three rows, the most interesting of which is the middle row, divided again by false octagonal pillars. The scenes are astronomical and potray the relationships between the heavens and their influence on humanity, starting with the life cycle, that is March during the Vernal Equinox. The dromedary, in April is proof of the taste for the exotic that was strong in Moretto's school. In the upper row, the constellations are portrayed according to the descriptions of Hyginus the ancient astronomer, and the character traits of persons born under the various signs. Below, there are two large sections that extend into the upper row with the *Virgin and the Twelve Apostles*; and finally the *Liberal and Mechanical Arts*.

In the Salone there is a huge *wooden horse* that was carved in 1466 on the occasion of a tournament, and it was based on an earlier statue by Donatello.

On the western wall is the *Monument to Livy* (1547) the ancient Roman historian born in Padua. The chiaroscuro frescoes around it have been attributed to Domenico Campagnola. And finally, there are other monuments commemorating famous citizens of Padua (Sperone Speroni, the erudite Renaissance man; Giovan Battista Belzoni, Egyptologist).

Palazzo della Ragione (Salone), the wooden horse.

Loggia della Gran Guardia,
façade.

Loggia della Gran Guardia,
interior.

LOGGIA DELLA GRAN GUARDIA

Due to the fire of 1420, the Maggior Consiglio was transferred to a building in this area. The old structure was quite drastically modified to meet the new needs, but it was only in 1545 that Falconetto managed to complete the work as we see it today. He created a building with a graceful portico on the ground floor façade, ahead of which is a high staircase, a long balustrade between the two stories and the typical Paduan series of openings: triple lighted and double lighted arched windows arranged symmetrically and made of Istrian stone.

Inside, the ceiling is divided into sixty five frescoed panels by Piero Antonio Torri (1667-68) representing *Scenes from the History of Padua*.

PALAZZO DEL CAPITANIO and THE ARCO DELL'OROLOGIO

Work on modernizing the façade of the **Palazzo del Capitanio** where one of the main magistrates of Padua lived was begun in 1599. A well defined balustrade and a cornice that begins at the upper part of the **Torre dell'Orologio** divides the façade into three rows, of which the lowest is rusticated. The piano nobile is embellished with Ionic pilaster strips against the doors that correspond to those above. In 1532 Falconetto modified the appearance of the triumphal archway-entrance. The great clock was completed in 1437 and the archway was embellished with Doric columns on high bases. In the arches are two *winged victories* and at the top, the *Lion of St. Mark*, and above that, two Ionic corner pillars frame the big clock.

Piazza dei Signori with the Palazzo del Capitanio and the Torre dell'Orologio, aerial view.

Palazzo del Capitanio and the Torre dell'Orologio (above); *Arco dell'Orologio* (below); **detail of the clock and the column with the Lion of St. Mark by Natale Sanavio** (opposite).

Corte Capitaniato (left);
the loggia in the Corte Capitaniato (right).

CORTE CAPITANIATO, LOGGIA DEL CAPITANIO and LIVIANO

After going through the Arco dell'Orologio, we come to the **Corte del Capitaniato** overlooked by the **Loggia del Capitaniato** that has been attributed to Andrea Moroni. It has three big, wide arches with rusticated pilaster strips and big windows. To the left of the court is the *Liviano*, home of various departments of the Faculty of Letters and Philosophy designed by Giò Ponti in 1939. From here we can go into the *Sala dei Giganti*, or room of the giants, all that remains of the former Carrara palace. In fact, all that we can see today of the XIV century painting cycle is the portrait of Petrach. What we actually see before us was executed in 1540 by Domenico Campagnola and his helpers. The coffered ceiling is decorated with floral friezes and inlays; the walls are adorned with portrayals of great kings and emperors and scenes from their lives.

LOGGIA CARRARESE

Loggia Carrarese.

Inside the perimeter that was once occupied by the Carrara palace (the Carrara were the Medieval lords of Padua) is the fourteenth century (1343) **Loggia**. This interesting architectural survivor may have been designed by Domenico da Firenze. The attribution is based on the fact that the Veronese red marble columns support the wooden ceiling beams in a decidedly Florentine manner (and during subsequent work and restorations on the ceiling over the centuries no changes were made, so that the Loggia could maintain its unique structure in this Paduan setting).

ARCO VALLARESSO

Situated between a courtyard in the Palace and Piazza Duomo, this is a triumphal arch built according to ancient models. It was erected after the plague of 1630 in honor of Captain Alvise Vallaresso who had distinguished himself in caring for the people. It was designed in 1632, probably by Giovan Battista della Scala, to models based on Palladio's plans, but revisited in light of seventeenth century tastes for stark chiaroscuro effects (as we can see in the protrusions and recesses). The plaque atop the arch commemorates Vallaresso's aid to the citizenry.

The door leading from the Corte Vallaresso to the Corte Capitaniato.

Arco Vallaresso.

Corte Vallaresso.

Monte di Pietà.

MONTE DI PIETÀ

Fresco in the loggia of the Monte di Pietà.

Alongside of the arch is the **Palazzo del Monte di Pietà**. It was created between 1531 and 1535 by Giovanni Maria Falconetto who rebuilt old Carrara family houses. The architect raised part of the building and imposed a typically sixteenth century rhythm on the six-arch façade; the last three that face towards the square date from 1611. In 1534 Domenico Campagnola did the frescoes depicting *Scenes from the Life of the Blessed Bernardino da Feltre* in the arcade. Other frescoes were added in the XVII century and the fifteenth century ones were restored. The façade overlooking Via Monte di Pietà by Vincenzo Dotto dates from 1613. It is distinguished by a slightly protruding portion with large columns that frame the impressivve doorway and support the statues of *Saint Bernardino* and *Charity*. The wings flanking the central part of the façade have large windows with rusticated pillars.

CATHEDRAL and BAPTISTRY

Cathedral, apse.

The **Cathedral**, dedicated to *Santa Maria Assunta* stands on the site where the Bishop Tricidio established the seat of the Paduan bishopric at the beginning of the IX-X century (if not in the IV-V century) at the intersection of the cardo and the decuman, the main roads that characterized the ancient city. In 1401 Francesco Novello da Carrara donated the area of the current square, as we can see from the inscription on the column that stands at the side. The area had been the market place and he donated it to Cathedral to build the cemetry. A competition was launched in 1547 to remodel the old church. It was won by Andrea da Valle, but the defeated Jacopo Sansovino submitted another plan and in the end the building was designed by several architects. Michelangelo had the idea for the apse, even though it was finally built to plans by Da Valle (1552). The transept was designed by Giulio Viola (1592), and the dome by Squarcina. The right arm by Almarigoto (1632) and the left by Paolo and Francesco Tentori (1702) while the only part of Frigimelica's façade (1730) that was built was the base as we can see today. The fact that so many different architects worked on the cathedral over a span of two hundred years has yielded a building without unity and many uncertainties in the "assembly" of the various sections.

Cathedral, façade.

Cathedral, second altar on the right.

Cathedral, interior.

Cathedral, Parodi, wooden pulpit (1692).

Nearly all the paintings inside the cathedral date from the XVIII century. Highlights are *the monument to the Bishop Tricidio* on the right wall of the vestibule that leads to the left part of the transept; on the same wall is the fifteenth century *Monument to Pietro Barocci Bishop of Padua,* by Tullio Lombardo. The outstanding artworks include the Baroque bronze gate to the presbytry and the *Virgin and Child* (apse of the right arm of the transept) which tradition maintains belonged to Petrarch. On the western wall of the Canon's Vestry are canvases by Domenico Campagnola dated 1564 portraying *Christ between Aaron and Melchizedek* and a big *reliquary* dated 1563.

Baptistry, façade.

Plaque over a tomb by Jacopo Dondi dell'Orologio, that was originally inside the Baptistry.

The **Baptistry**, dedicated to Saint John stands to the right of the cathedral; it was built over the site of an earlier baptistry in 1260. The central part has a square plan topped by a dome built on a high drum; the apse, which protrudes was counterbalanced by a vestibule (narthex) that was destroyed in the XVI century. The interior is richly decorated with paintings that were completed in 1378. They have been attributed to Giusto de' Menabuoi, who did the frescoes in the Baptistry in Florence. The reason for this attribution is that many Florentine exiles who lived in Padua in the XIV century met here. On the dome we see *Christ* and the *Virgin*; the five registers are decorated with scenes of *Paradise* with the hierarchies of angels, the *Apostles*, and the *Saints*, and then *Scenes from the Book of Genesis*. On the pendentives that support the dome are the *Evangelists* and the *Prophets*; the walls are decorated with *Scenes from the New Testament*, and scenes from the *Apocalypse* in the apse complete this Biblical cycle that has few equals anywhere.

ORATORIO DEI COLOMBINI and PALAZZO PAPAFAVA

The **Oratorio dei Colombini** stands in Via dei Papafava; it was expanded in 1686 and then again in the XIX century. It consists of a single room preceded by a vestibule with Ionic columns. It has a low, arched ceiling and a door at the rear that leads into the palace gardens. The gardens were redesigned by Jappelli in the nineteenth century in the English naturalistic style. In middle of the garden is a well. According to legend St. Anthony's breviary fell into the well and was taken out, dried and returned to him by angels .

At the corner of Via Marsala, stands the **Palace**, that the **Papafava** bought in the early XIX century and had modeled in the Neoclassical fashion–both inside and out–starting in 1807. A high ashlar base is surmounted by Corinthian columns which are placed in relation to the large salon. The main door (in Via Marsala) leads into a large atrium with a coffered ceiling and big Tuscan-style columns. A wide double staircase with a balustrade decorated with floral patterns rises from this lobby. In the salon on the piano nobile, there are plaster works attributed to Canova and a *Neoclassical suite* with several round rooms and salons decorated with scenes from the *Iliad*, painted by Giovanni De Min. All the accessories (furniture, chandeliers, figurines, etc.) are copies of Roman items.

Bishop's Palace, façade (left); *aedicula above the entrance to the Bishop's Palace; the inscription identifies the figures as Henry IV and Queen Berthe* (right).

BISHOP'S PALACE

Arcades in Via Vescovado.

The **Bishop's Palace** was built over Medieval structures (in Via Duomo and Via Vescovado we can still see sections of old 'though not all original' crenelations of the walls) and over an ancient Roman *palatium publicum*. The building was almost totally rebuilt by Lorenzo da Bologna in 1485 and was last restored in 1950. The impressive building is essentially a cube that conveys the idea of the great fortress that once stood on this site. A series of loggias were added starting the sixteenth century. On the Via Vandelli side they consist of ashlar pillars from the XVII and XVIII centuries; on the Piazza Duomo side they date from the XVIII century. Inside, on the first floor, there are the XV century frescoes in the *Sala Grande* portraying emperors and floral motifs; there is also Jacopo da Montagnana's *Resurrection*. In the *Sala dei Vescovi* (or Bishops' Room) on the upper floor are Montagnana's portraits of the bishops of Padua up to 1494; and above one of the doors is a sixteenth century roundel *Portrait of Petrarch* (it was originally in the poet's house which has since been torn down). This room leads to the chapel frescoed by Montagnana in 1494; the colored ceramic floor is a noteworthy feature of the chapel.

PALAZZO DEGLI SPECCHI

This building has long been believed to have been the home of Livy because in a groundfloor room there was an ancient marble bust that was thought to be that of the historian. Domenico Campagnola painted allegorical scenes related to the life of this illustrious Paduan. Although the façade was considerably modified during the nineteenth century, the *courtyard* is extremely interesting because of its sixteenth century painting that encompasses Medieval and fifteenth century elements, and statuary that may be by Ammannati.

PORTA SAN GIOVANNI

This massive structure was built by Falconetto in 1528, as we can see from the architect's signature over the door. It is characterized by Corinthian semi-coloumns on high pedestals on the first floor and pilaster strips on the second framing a *lion of St. Mark* of which only traces remain today as it was probably carved in the XVIII century. The façade of the door facing the city serves is divided in two registers, each of which is embellished by pilaster strips. On the side of the door opening towards the countryside the lower register has semi-columns rather than pilaster strips. The aim was to emphasize the the value of the triumphal entrance for those entering the city.

Palazzo degli Specchi, façade.

Porta San Giovanni (opposite page).

San Nicolò, façade (left);
Teatro Verdi (right).

San Nicolò, façade with the remains of the XV century decorations (above); *Roman relief carving of a deer* (below).

TEATRO VERDI or TEATRO NUOVO

The theater was built in 1748 to plans by Antonio Cugini; the outside was later remodelled according to Giuseppe Jappelli's designs. The semicircular façade is most impressive with its arcades topped by richly decorated windows and round oculi.

CHURCH OF SAN NICOLÒ

This church was established in 1090, the façade today is like that of a basilica with a rose window and the central portion that is higher than the lateral naves. The portal is typical of the late fifteenth century Lombard school with richly decorated lateral pilaster strips (*candelabra*). Only the part left of the entrance is what remains of the original structure, with pendentive Lombard style arches and two stone panels with relief carvings of *deer*. Inside the architecture is exquisitely fourteenth century, with huge cross vaults. The Tuscan Renaissance columns reveal the modernization that the building had undergone. To the left is the Medieval *chapel of the Forzatè* which is now used as a baptistry; at the rear there is a sarcophagus which, too, is decorated with deer and spiral columns. The *Virgin and Child with Saints* in the apse is by Giandomenico Tiepolo (1777). On the side of the left nave, in the last chapel inside the eighteenth century altar there is a *Virgin and Child* by an unknown, late fifteenth century artist who had been in contact with Antonello da Messina. In the next to the last chapel there are four wood bas-relief carvings depicting *Scenes from the Lives of the Saints* (XVI century).

CHURCH OF SANTA LUCIA or
DELL'ADORAZIONE PERPETUA and
ORATORY OF SAN ROCCO

The **church of Santa Lucia** dates from the X century, however, the way it appears today is typical of eighteenth century restorations and reconstructions. Tall columns with richly decorated capitals and the large central door with its circular front (1711-1726) embellish the façade. Inside, majestic semi-columns against the walls alternate blind parts and altars with many statues that provide a significant overview of eighteenth century tastes in sculpture in the Veneto region. Left of the presbytry is a fine *St. Luke* by Giambattista Tiepolo; below the first arch of the vault is the *Presentation in the Temple* by Campagnola; the graceful composition of the carved *Angels* on the altar on the left wall could mean that it was done by Antonio Bonazza; the *Incredulity of St. Thomas* (1610) an early work by the painter, Alessandro Varotari known as Padovanino, situated in the first arch against the entrance is yet another wonderful example.

To the left of the church, looking at the façade is the **Oratory of San Rocco**, with a fine cycle of sixteenth century frescoes. Although they wereclumsily restored in the last century, there is still much to be admired in the *Scenes from the Life of San Rocco* by various artists including Campagnola.

Santa Lucia, interior.

Scuola di Santa Lucia, entrance.

CHURCH and SCHOOL OF SANTA MARIA DEL CARMINE or I CARMINI

The **church of Santa Maria del Carmine** is on the north side of Piazza Petrarca (Luigi Ceccon's 1874 *monument to Francesco Petrarca* graces the middle of this square). It was built in 1212 and then reconstructed by Lorenzo da Bologna in 1495; the big door dates from 1737, and the roofing of the dome was built between 1931-32 to repair the destruction caused by World War I bombing raids. The statues in the niches above the unfinished façade door are by Tommaso Bonazza.

Santa Maria del Carmine, façade.

Santa Maria del Carmine, interior.

Inside the church the vaulted ceiling dates from the XVII century; a colonnade with semi-circular arches divides the nave from the apse. Lavish, mostly seventeenth century, decorations characterize the church; the highlights are the fourth chapel on the left (1562-63); the decorations on the dome and pendentives date from 1933-34 and were done by Antonio Fasal. The high altar was built in 1813 under the direction of Antonio Noale, with *angels* by Rinaldo Rinaldi. On the sixth altar to the right, starting from the entrance, is a painting of *Christ and the Mother of the Zebedees,* by Padovanino.

Next to the church in Piazza Petrarca, is the **Scuola del Carmine** with a fine cycle of frescoes that has been partly attributed to Domenico Campagnola. In the third panel on the right in the scene of the *Wedding of the Virgin* is a *portrait of Albrecht Dürer*, the XVI century German artist whom Campagnola greatly admired.

Synagogue (above) and *the Old Jewish Ghetto.*

The synagogue.

THE GHETTO and SYNAGOGUE

Although there had been a flourishing Jewish community in Padua as early as the XIII century, it was only in the sixteenth that they were forced into a ghetto which was then closed off by four gates in 1603. At Via San Martino 9 stands the most important **synagogue** that was built in 1548 and then reconstructed several times with a stone façade. Inside, the single room is divided into two sections, the *tevah* and the *aron* (for reading), for the Torah scrolls, as required by Jewish tradition. The aron with its black marble columns and six Corinthian columns and canopy is typically Baroque.

Around Padua

Panorama of Arquà.

Burchiello on the Brenta.

Padua's surroiundings are rich in history and various attractions, partly because of the Brenta River and the *"**Brenta Vecchia**" (commonly known as the **Riviera del Brenta**). Then there are also the Euganean Hills with their many hot springs. In fact, spas such as Abano have been popular since antiquity. Neither of the two rivers actually touch Padua, but there is a navigable canal, known as the Navile with a ferry (the **Burchiello**) that reaches the **riviera** after casting off from the **pontile Bassanello** in the city; the pontile has long been Padua's river dock.*

Riviera del Brenta,
Villa Velluti.

The shores of the Riviera are dotted with villas that are outstanding for their architecture and landscaping. At **STRA** *is the* **Villa Pisani** *on the left bank; it was started in 1720 and completed in 1756 and is famous for its gardens and frescoes by Giambattista Tiepolo. Next come the* **Villa Lazara Pisani** *and after the center of* **DOLO**, *on the right bank are the* **Villa Bon** *and the* **Palazzo Feretti-Mocenigo** *by Vincenzo Scamozzi. Then along the entire route, as far as the Venice Lagoon and Andrea Palladio's villa known as the* **Malcontenta** *there are stately country homes and estates. The Venetian nobility acquired these estates to invest their earnings from foreign trade and to farm the mainland.*

Stra, Villa Pisani.

Andrea Palladio's villa known as the Malcontenta.

The cathedral at Dolo, interior.

The Dolo cathedral, interior, detail of the ceiling.

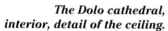

Villa Barbarigo.

The still intact natural beauties of the **Euganean Hills** are now (actually since 1989) protected by the **Parco Regionale** which should also enhance the thermal resources of the area while protecting the landscape and cultural assets. From Padua it is possible to circumnavitage the hills going towards **ABANO TERME**. The spa town was probably founded by Venetics around the V century B.C. The many spa establishments; villas and **Viale delle Terme** have given the town a decidedly late nineteenth century atmosphere. The old **Cathedral** has been remodelled and restored several times, up through the nineteen sixties.

Continuing through the hills, we come to **MONTEGROTTO TERME**, a spa town that has been known since ancient Roman times, and which, therefore, has a large and interesting **archeological area**.

Montegrotto Terme, archeological ruins from the Roman era.

Church of Santa Maria, façade.

Church of Santa Maria, interior.

ARQUÀ PETRARCA, *is a renowned resort in the Euganean hills, with a fine Medieval fabric along the hills. Due to its healthful climate, this second home of the Venetian nobility was settled mainly between the XV and XVI centuries. Some of the outstanding buildings include the Venetian Gothic* **Palazzo Contarini**, *and* **Casa Pestrin**, *used as an olive pressing facility, has traces of colored geometric patterns on the façade.*
Another point of interest at Arquà is **Petrarch's tomb**. *The poet moved here during the final period of his life (1370 to 1374). He is buried in the yard of the town's main church,* **Santa Maria** *just as he wished. The monument is made of red marble from Verona, in an early Christian style; the bronze bust was added by Pietro Paolo Valdezocco of Padua in the second half of the XV century.*

INDEX

BIBLIOGRAPHY

- Alvise Corarno e il suo tempo, Catalogue, Padua, 1980
- La Basilica di Santa Giustina in Padua, Arte e Storia, Castel Franco Veneto, 1970
- AA.VV., Il complesso di San Francesco Grande in Padova. Storia e Arte, Padua 1983
- AA.VV., Il Duomo di Padova e il suo Battistero, Trieste, 1977
- C. Bellinati-L.Puppi (a cura di), Padova. Basiliche e Chiese, Padua, 1975
- D. Bertizzolo (a cura di), La chiesa di Santa Sofia in Padova, Cittadella, 1982
- S. Bettini-L.Puppi, La Chiesa degli Eremitani, Vicenza, 1970
- S. Polano, Guida all'architettura italiana del Novecento, Milan, 1991
- L. Puppi, Andrea Palladio, Milan, 1972
- L. Puppi, Padova, Rome-Bari, 1982
- L. Puppi- L. Toffanin, Guida di Padova. Arte e storia tra vie e piazze, Trieste, 1983
- L. Puppi-F. Zuliani (a cura di), Padova. case e Palazzi, Vicenza, 1977
- A. Ventura, Padova, Bari, 1989
- R. Wittkower, L'influenza del Palladio sullo sviluppo dell'architettura religiosa veneziana nel Sei e Settecento, in «Bollettino CISA», 1963, V, pp.61-86

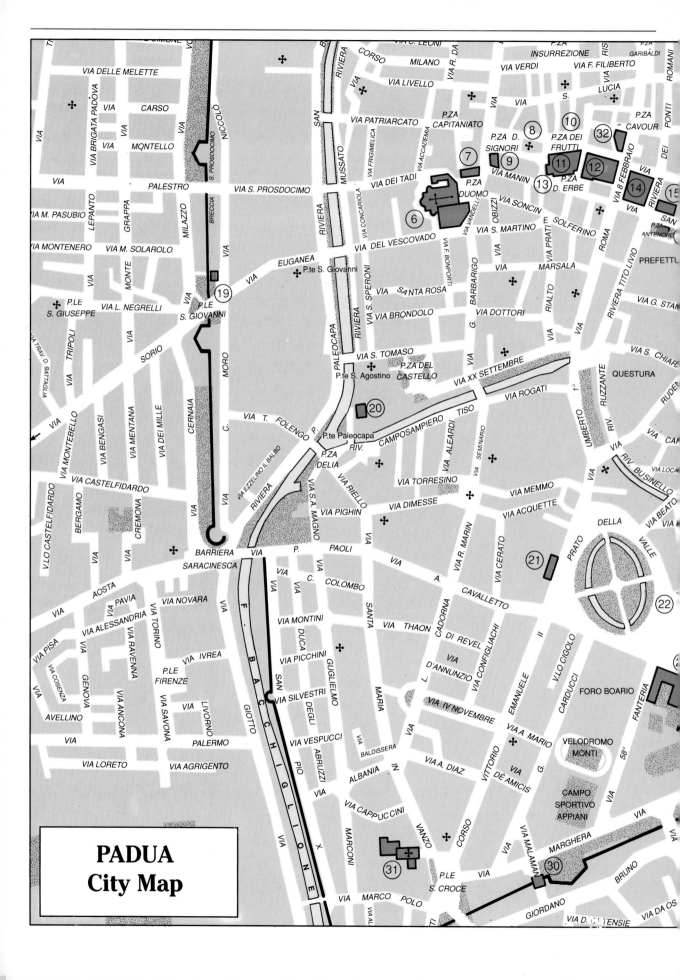

PADUA
City Map

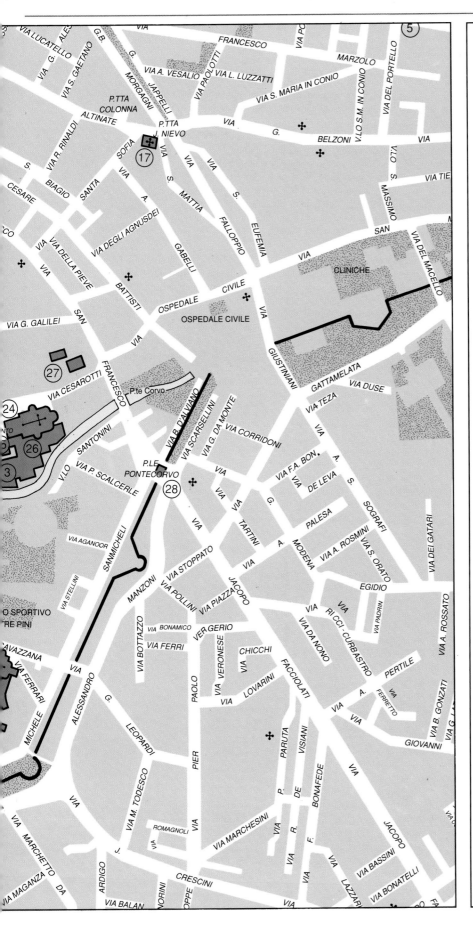